QL
31
.F65
N53
2002

CLEARI

W9-BAJ-823

R0400417081

Dian Fossey : primatologist

DEC - - 2003

Chicago Public Library
Clearing Branch
6423 West 63rd Place
Chicago, Illinois 60638-5005

WOMEN in SCIENCE

Dian Fossey

Primatologist

Women in Science

Rachel Carson
Author/Ecologist

Dian Fossey
Primatologist

Jane Goodall
Primatologist/Naturalist

Maria Goeppert Mayer
Physicist

Barbara McClintock
Geneticist

Maria Mitchell
Astronomer

WOMEN in SCIENCE

Dian Fossey

Primatologist

Lois P. Nicholson

CHELSEA HOUSE
PUBLISHERS
A Haights Cross Communications Company
Philadelphia

CHELSEA HOUSE PUBLISHERS

VP, NEW PRODUCT DEVELOPMENT Sally Cheney
DIRECTOR OF PRODUCTION Kim Shinners
CREATIVE MANAGER Takeshi Takahashi
MANUFACTURING MANAGER Diann Grasse

Staff for DIAN FOSSEY

EDITOR Patrick M. N. Stone
PRODUCTION EDITOR Jaimie Winkler
PHOTO EDITOR Sarah Bloom
SERIES & COVER DESIGNER Terry Mallon
LAYOUT 21st Century Publishing and Communications, Inc.

©2003 by Chelsea House Publishers, a subsidiary of Haights Cross Communications.
All rights reserved. Printed and bound in the United States of America.

A Haights Cross Communications ⌐ Company

http://www.chelseahouse.com

First Printing

1 3 5 7 9 8 6 4 2

Library of Congress Cataloging-in-Publication Data

Nicholson, Lois, 1949–
    Dian Fossey / Lois P. Nicholson.
        p. cm.—(Women in science)
Summary: Profiles the life of the scientist who studied mountain gorillas
in central Africa and worked to ensure their survival.
    ISBN 0-7910-6907-9
    1. Fossey, Dian—Juvenile literature. 2. Primatologists—United
States—Biography—Juvenile literature. [1. Fossey, Dian. 2. Zoologists.
3. Scientists. 4. Women—Biography. 5. Gorilla.] I. Title. II. Series:
Women in science (Chelsea House Publishers)
QL31.F65 N53 2002
599.884'092—dc21
                                                        2002015592

R0400417081

Table of Contents

Chicago Public Library
Clearing Branch
6423 West 63rd Place
Chicago, Illinois 60638-5005

Introduction

Jill Sideman, Ph.D.
President, Association for Women in Science

I am honored to introduce WOMEN IN SCIENCE, **a continuing series** of books about great women who pursued their interests in various scientific fields, often in the face of barriers erected by the societies in which they lived, and who have won the highest accolades for their achievements. I myself have been a scientist for well over 40 years and am at present the president of the Association for Women in Science, a national organization formed over 30 years ago to support women in choosing and advancing in scientific careers. I am actively engaged in environmental science as a vice-president of a very large engineering firm that has offices all around the world. I work with many different types of scientists and engineers from all sorts of countries and cultures. I have been able to observe myself the difficulties that many girls and women face in becoming active scientists, and how they overcome those difficulties. The women scientists who are the subject of this series undoubtedly experienced both the great excitement of scientific discovery and the often blatant discrimination and discouragement offered by society in general and during their elementary, high school, and college education in particular. Many of these women grew up in the United States during the twentieth century, receiving their scientific education in American schools and colleges, and practicing their science in American universities. It is interesting to think about their lives and successes in science in the context of the general societal view of women as scientists that prevailed during their lifetimes. What barriers did they face? What factors in their lives most influenced their interest in science, the development of their analytical skills, and their determination to carry on with their scientific careers? Who were their role models and encouraged them to pursue science?

Let's start by looking briefly at the history of women as scientists in the United States. Until the end of the 1800s, not just in the United States but in European cultures as well, girls and women were expected to be interested in and especially inclined toward science. Women wrote popular science books and scientific textbooks and presented science using female characters. They attended scientific meetings and published in scientific journals.

In the early part of the twentieth century, though, the relationship of women to science in the United States began to change. The scientist was seen as cerebral, impersonal, and even competitive, and the ideal woman diverged from this image; she was expected to be docile, domestic, delicate, and unobtrusive, to focus on the home and not engage in science as a profession.

From 1940 into the 1960s, driven by World War II and the Cold War, the need for people with scientific training was high and the official U.S. view called for women to pursue science and engineering. But women's role in science was envisioned not as primary researcher, but as technical assistant, laboratory worker, or schoolteacher, and the public thought of women in the sciences as unattractive, unmarried, and thus unfulfilled. This is the prevailing public image of women in science even today.

Numerous studies have shown that for most of the twentieth century, throughout the United States, girls have been actively discouraged from taking science and mathematics courses throughout their schooling. Imagine the great mathematical physicist and 1963 Nobel laureate Maria Goeppert Mayer being told by her high school teachers that "girls don't need math or physics," or Barbara McClintock, the winner of the 1983 Nobel Prize in Medicine or Physiology who wrote on the fundamental laws of gene and chromosome behavior, hearing comments that "girls are not suited to science"! Yet statements like these were common and are made even today.

I personally have experienced discouragement of this kind, as have many of my female scientist friends.

I grew up in a small rural town in southern Tennessee and was in elementary and high school between 1944 and 1956. I vividly remember the day the principal of the high school came to talk to my eighth-grade class about the experience of high school and the subjects we would be taking. He said, "Now, you girls, you don't need to take algebra or geometry, since all the math you'll need to know will be how to balance a checkbook." I was stunned! When I told my mother, my role model and principal encourager, she was outraged. We decided right then that I would take four years of mathematics in high school, and it became my favorite subject—especially algebra and geometry.

I've mentioned my mother as my role model. She was born in 1911 in the same small Southern town and has lived there her entire life. She was always an unusual personality. A classic tomboy, she roamed the woods throughout the county, conducting her own observational wildlife studies and adopting orphaned birds, squirrels, and possums. In high school she took as many science classes as she could. She attended the University of Tennessee in Knoxville for two years, the only woman studying electrical engineering. Forced by financial problems to drop out, she returned home, married, and reared five children, of whom I'm the oldest. She remained fascinated by science, especially biology. When I was in the fourth grade, she brought an entire pig's heart to our school to demonstrate how the heart is constructed to make blood circulate; one of my classmates fainted, and even the teacher turned pale.

In later years, she adapted an electronic device for sensing the moisture on plant leaves—the Electronic Leaf, invented by my father for use in wholesale commercial nurseries—to a smaller scale and sold it all over the world as part of a home nursery system. One of the proudest days of her life was when I received my Ph.D. in physical and inorganic chemistry,

specializing in quantum mechanics—there's the love of mathematics again! She encouraged and pushed me all the way
through my education and scientific career. I imagine that she
was just like the father of Maria Mitchell, one of the outstanding
woman scientists profiled in the first season of this series.
Mitchell (1818–1889) learned astronomy from her father,
surveying the skies with him from the roof of their Nantucket
house. She discovered a comet in 1847, for which discovery she
received a medal from the King of Denmark. She went on to
become the first director of Vassar College Observatory in 1865
and in this position created the earliest opportunities for women
to study astronomy at a level that prepared them for professional
careers. She was inspired by her father's love of the stars.

I remember hearing Jane Goodall speak in person when
I was in graduate school in the early 1960s. At that time she had
just returned to the United States from the research compound
she established in Tanzania, where she was studying the social
dynamics of chimpanzee populations. Here was a young woman,
only a few years older than I, who was dramatically changing
the way in which people thought about primate behavior. She
was still in graduate school then—she completed her Ph.D. in
1965. Her descriptions of her research findings started me on a
lifetime avocation for ethology—the study of human, animal,
and even insect populations and their behaviors. She remains a
role model for me today.

And I must just mention Rachel Carson, a biologist whose
book *Silent Spring* first brought issues of environmental
pollution to the attention of the majority of Americans. Her
work fueled the passage of the National Environmental Policy
Act in 1969; this was the first U.S. law aimed at restoring and
protecting the environment. Rachel Carson helped create the
entire field of environmental studies that has been the focus of
my scientific career since the early 1970s.

Women remain a minority in scientific and technological
fields in the United States today, especially in the "hard science"

fields of physics and engineering, of whose populations women represent only 12%. This became an increasing concern during the last decade of the 20th century as industries, government, and academia began to realize that the United States was falling behind in developing sufficient scientific and technical talent to meet the demand. In 1999–2000, I served on the National Commission on the Advancement of Women and Minorities in Science, Engineering, and Technology (CAWMSET); this commission was established through a 1998 congressional bill sponsored by Constance Morella, a congresswoman from Maryland. CAWMSET's purpose was to analyze the reasons why women and minorities continue to be underrepresented in science, engineering, and technology and to recommend ways to increase their participation in these fields. One of the CAWMSET findings was that girls and young women seem to lose interest in science at two particular points in their pre-college education: in middle school and in the last years of high school—points that may be especially relevant to readers of this series.

An important CAWMSET recommendation was the establishment of a national body to undertake and oversee the implementation of all CAWMSET recommendations, including those that are aimed at encouraging girls and young women to enter and stay in scientific disciplines. That national body has been established with money from eight federal agencies and both industry and academic institutions; it is named BEST (Building Engineering and Science Talent). BEST sponsored a Blue-Ribbon Panel of experts in education and science to focus on the science and technology experiences of young women and minorities in elementary, middle, and high school; the panel developed specific planned actions to help girls and young women become and remain interested in science and technology. This plan of action was presented to Congress in September of 2002. All of us women scientists fervently hope that BEST's plans will be implemented successfully.

I want to impress on all the readers of this series, too, that it is never too late to engage in science. One of my professional friends, an industrial hygienist who specializes in safety and health issues in the scientific and engineering workplace, recently told me about her grandmother. This remarkable woman, who had always wanted to study biology, finally received her bachelor's degree in that discipline several years ago—at the age of 94.

The scientists profiled in WOMEN IN SCIENCE are fascinating women who throughout their careers made real differences in scientific knowledge and the world we all live in. I hope that readers will find them as interesting and inspiring as I do.

1

Murder
in the Mist

Dian Fossey loved Christmas. Ten thousand feet up in the Virunga Mountains of Africa, the wreath adorning the door of her corrugated-metal hut featured a Santa Claus of red felt bearing a sign that said "Howdy." A small bit of decoration, perhaps—but it reveals much about the complex woman who dwelt inside late in 1985. Those who worked with Fossey knew her as demanding and difficult, with both coworkers and local officials. She rarely allowed others to see her other self—the wickedly funny Dian who loved social events and who, like a child, secretly craved acceptance from others.

Fossey's annual Christmas festivities included a giant heather tree decorated with tin foil, popcorn, candles, and flowers. In 1985, this was surrounded by carefully wrapped gifts Fossey had purchased while visiting the United States. Each gift had been selected with care. The celebration featured carols sung in English, French, and Kinyarwanda, the language

Karlsoke, the isolated camp in the Virungas that Fossey had worked so hard to establish, would become the site of her death. It is shown here shrouded in the Virungan mist that has become an integral part of the Fossey legend.

of the local Rwandans, and a generous feast of meats washed down with *urwagwa*, the local banana beer. As many as 100 guests—associates, neighbors, and workers and their families from her primate research center, Karisoke—crowded into Fossey's camp for the holiday party. But the celebration had been postponed until New Year's Day to coincide with an American film crew's anticipated arrival later that week.

Two of Karisoke's visiting graduate students dined with Fossey that evening: Wayne McGuire, a young American who was working on his doctorate in anthropology, studying the male gorilla's role in caring for the infants of a community, and Joseph Munyaneza, a Rwandan zoology major. The students hoped that the holiday spirit would lighten Fossey's usual ranting mood. But it didn't. Fossey pointedly questioned their research methodology while the trio shared a meal of lamb.

Since arriving in Africa in 1963, Fossey had become the world's foremost authority on the largest and rarest of the great apes, the mountain gorilla. Although Fossey had come to the Virunga Mountains for scientific study of these magnificent beasts, her role of scientist had evolved into that of zealous or even militant conservationist. She realized that unless the gorillas were saved from extinction, studying them would be futile. Two decades earlier, over 400 gorillas had lived in the mountains. By 1985, despite Fossey's courageous, often daring attempts to save them, only about 220 remained.

As an unhappy, lonely child in California, Fossey had had an affinity for animals, but her parents, who seem to have suppressed much of the joy of Fossey's childhood, discouraged her longing for a pet. Later, as a trained scientist, she brought her childlike love of animals to the study of the great apes, an evolutionary family that includes gorillas, chimpanzees, orangutans, and bonobos.

Unlike most male primatologists before her, Fossey saw the gorillas as individuals. Like her contemporary Jane Goodall, whose pioneering study of chimpanzees in Tanzania preceded Fossey's arrival on the continent, Fossey brought a woman's perspective to scientific observation. As Goodall had done with chimps, Fossey gave each primate a name—Uncle Bert, Flossie, Pango, Puck—and described them as individuals capable of experiencing emotions, instead of mere research subjects. Goodall's and Fossey's controversial techniques met with scrutiny from the male-dominated scientific community. Despite their colleagues' skepticism, they persevered.

Interest in the plight of African wildlife had steadily increased since the publication in 1960 of *Born Free*, a highly successful novel by Joy Adamson, an Austrian wildlife advocate who lived in Kenya. Adamson's work with lions awakened the Western world to the mounting, critical loss of wildlife and habitat in Africa.

Adamson had been killed by wildlife poachers in 1980.

Like Adamson, Goodall and Fossey had devoted much of their lives to observing their subjects in the field; but by 1985 Fossey was depending more and more on her staff for news of her beloved gorilla clans. A chain-smoker who consumed three packs of cigarettes each day, Fossey suffered from advanced emphysema, a deterioration of the lungs, that was aggravated by the mountain's altitude, cold, and dampness. Her legs were weak, and hairline fractures in her feet prevented her from walking any great distance. Fossey's poor health had prevented her from visiting the primates in the field since September. When the two male students visited on that Christmas night, she was eager for news.

As the evening wore on, Fossey, who was also a heavy drinker, lapsed into her habit of berating her coworkers. She vehemently criticized her dinner guests' scientific techniques and accused them of caring more about their research than about protecting gorillas from attack by poachers, who killed the huge gorillas and sold their remains in foreign markets. The persistent slaughter of the gorillas intensified Fossey's critical attitude toward the camp's volunteers, and she had developed a reputation for questioning the loyalty of Karisoke's student workers. She measured an individual's commitment toward gorilla conservation against her own demanding, self-sacrificing, often fanatical standards. Still, when the dinner ended, just before the two men returned to their tents for the night, Fossey presented them with Christmas gifts. They were glad to escape Fossey's tirade, but they regretted having no gifts for her.

McGuire and Munyaneza spent the next day in the field, counting the local groups of 70 gorillas. That evening, McGuire stopped by Fossey's green metal hut to relate his findings. An insomniac who often worked well into the morning hours, Fossey was lying on her bed, her six-foot frame sprawled comfortably across its expanse as smoke curled from the ever-present cigarette between her fingers. The kerosene

Dian Fossey ran the research institute at Karisoke, in what is now the Democratic Republic of the Congo, from 1967 until her murder in 1985. "When you realize the value of all life," she wrote, "you dwell less on what is past and concentrate on the preservation of the future."

lamp illuminated her two pet African gray parrots, Dot and Dash, the straw mats covering the metal walls, and the books that filled her bookcase: Darwin's *On the Origin of Species*, Isak Denison's *Out of Africa*, Livingstone's *Lost and Found*, *The Reader's Digest Fix-It-Yourself Manual*, and *Teach Yourself Swahili*. Cherished tools of Fossey's work surrounded her: a manual typewriter and numerous black-and-white photographs of her gorilla family. McGuire said goodnight and retreated in the darkness to his tent, a mere 100 yards away.

McGuire's sleep abruptly ended early the next morning when the Swahili cries from Kanyaragana, Fossey's house servant, filled the frigid morning air. "*Fossey kufa, Fossey kufa!*"

("Fossey's dead! Fossey's dead!") Following Kanyaragana, McGuire rushed to the tin hut, where he discovered Fossey's body on the floor next to her bed. Near her blood-covered remains lay her handgun; an unused clip of ammunition rested beside it. "The place was a mess," McGuire later recalled. "Things were thrown around. Her head was covered with blood. When I reached down to check her vital signs, I saw her face had been split, diagonally, with one machete blow." (Brower and Vollers, 46)

Someone had entered Fossey's cabin between McGuire's departure on the previous night and the invisible dawn of December 27. The killer had cut a hole in the sheet-metal siding of the cabin, removed the *panga* (machete) that hung on the wall near the door, and used that machete to murder Fossey. American and African money lay in plain view, untouched. Nothing had been taken except her life.

Thus began many years of mystery surrounding the death of Dian Fossey. Those who had known her the longest guessed that one of the poachers whom she had pursued, threatened, tortured, or imprisoned over the years had exacted revenge; two suspects were apprehended and exonerated. The truth about Fossey's death would not emerge for a decade.

But the tragedy of her death has done nothing to diminish the value of her work; if anything, it has brought to her cause even greater exposure. In addition to knowledge of the gorillas, the primates believed closest to humans in terms of behavior, Dian Fossey established the importance and principles of conservation that have resulted not only in saving the great apes from extinction, but also in enabling their population to swell to the hundreds since 1985. Her datebook's final entry best expresses the irony surrounding her untimely death: "When you realize the value of all life, you dwell less on what is past and concentrate on the preservation of the future."

In the end, the Gorilla Girl, *Nyiramachabelli*—"the lady who lives alone in the forest"—had triumphed after all.

2

Going to Meet the Gorillas: 1932–1963

AN EARLY PREFERENCE FOR ANIMALS

Dian Fossey's early childhood, spent near San Francisco in the 1930s, was a lonely one. She hardly knew her father, George, who struggled to earn a living as an insurance salesman during the Great Depression. George Fossey's financial problems led to his immoderate consumption of alcohol; he and his wife were divorced in 1935, when Dian was three years old, and Dian seldom saw or heard from her father after that.

Kitty Fossey, Dian's mother, was a petite woman whom some described as the most attractive fashion model in San Francisco. Dian seldom saw her, spending most of her time with her mother's sister, Aunt Flossie, and Flossie's husband, Uncle Bert; they became Dian's favorite family members, and she would maintain a close relationship with them throughout her life. When Dian was five years old, her mother remarried. Her new stepfather, Richard Price, was a successful building

The thought of going on safari intrigued Fossey, and she mortgaged her income for years, and relied on a friend, for the means to make the journey possible. Already in her fourth decade of life when she left, she found her mission in Africa: studying and working to preserve the mountain gorillas.

contractor and socialite. Price became the only father Fossey ever knew, and she called him "Daddy," but he never officially adopted her.

A stern parent, Price enforced strict household rules and showed his stepdaughter little attention. Until she was 10, Dian was permitted to dine with her parents only on holidays and special occasions. Usually, she dined with the housekeeper in the family's kitchen. Her stepfather later explained, "I had always been brought up to think that children dined with adults when they were becoming adults." (Mowat, 2)

An only child with no friends, Dian craved affection; but the Prices seemed oblivious to their daughter's emotional needs. Like many children, she longed for a pet, but her parents consistently refused to let her have one. They did relent once, though, and allow her a goldfish. One day she found it floating dead in the water and was devastated. "I cried for a week," she later wrote in her journal. "A friend at school offered me a hamster, but they [her parents] considered it dirty, so that was out." (Mowat, 2)

Throughout her childhood, Dian's greatest joy was the horseback riding lessons her stepfather provided for her at a nearby riding academy. She adored being around the tall horses, talking to them, learning to handle and ride them. She eventually became active in her high school riding club and owned her own horse. She felt that the pets and animals she loved, and shared a strong kinship with, accepted her unconditionally. She was at ease in their company, and this early preference for and bond with animals would determine the course of her life.

Dian rapidly grew to be much taller than her mother, a diminutive blonde, and was six feet tall by the age of 14. She towered over her ninth-grade classmates, most of whom were a foot shorter. Her rough-hewn face, framed with thick, long, black hair, and her heavy, dark eyebrows combined to make her look very different from other teens. Although some found her appearance agreeably striking, Dian thought her height and intense features made her look freakish. Feeling awkward and unattractive, she grew increasingly shy and introverted.

After Dian's graduation from Atherton's Lowell High

The time Fossey spent working on a ranch in Montana affirmed her love of open spaces and her close relationship with the natural world. She seems to have felt more at home in the wild than with humans—a part of her character that made her well-suited to the life's work she finally chose.

School in 1949 at the age of 17, she attended Marin Junior College in Kentfield, California. At Marin, with her stepfather's encouragement, she enrolled in business courses, but she soon came to hate them. Her parents provided little financial support. Instead, the girl's aunt and uncle, Flossie and Bert, helped her when she needed money.

In addition to taking classes, Dian worked as a machine operator in a factory and a clerk in a department store. Later, she spent a summer working as a ranch hand at a Montana dude ranch. There she discovered another important aspect of her nature: she thrived in Montana's open spaces, where the earth and sky seemed eternal. The San Francisco "city girl" felt most at peace with animals in the wild.

In 1950, Dian cast aside her stepfather's wishes and enrolled in a pre-veterinarian program at the University of California at Davis. Although she loved animals, Dian was not a strong student in the sciences. She struggled with physics and chemistry. After two years, her poor grades made admission to the veterinary school unlikely.

Disappointed, Dian once more altered her career plans, turning her interest to handicapped children. She transferred to San Jose State College, which was near her San Francisco home, and enrolled in occupational therapy courses. When she graduated in 1954 with a degree in occupational therapy, she set her sights beyond California to find a job. An advertisement appeared for a director of an occupational therapy program at Kosair Crippled Children's Hospital in Louisville, Kentucky. Not only far from California and her parents, Kentucky was horse country—and Dian still loved to ride.

THE FIRST THOUGHT OF AFRICA

Kosair Hospital was small; only two doctors and five nurses worked there. Most of the children were victims of polio, stricken before the discovery of the Salk vaccine. They needed help both learning to walk with braces on their legs and using their hands to perform tasks. Other Kosair patients had autism, a neurological disorder affecting a child's ability to communicate, understand language, and relate to others. "These children have a variety of physical and emotional disabilities and are lost in this world of ours," Fossey wrote in her journal. "They need a tremendous amount of care and kindness to make them feel life is worth living." (Mowat, 3)

Fossey was as comfortable with the children as she was

with animals. But she was also tough, and demanded that they push themselves and work hard to overcome disabilities caused by their weakened limbs. Some patients disliked her steely approach, while others responded to her caring, respect, and love.

Fossey's coworkers found her distant. She seemed indifferent to their overtures of friendship and made no effort to develop relationships with staff members. If her coworkers attempted to get to know her, Fossey discouraged their efforts. Consequently, most of them left her alone. There was one employee who made the effort: Mary Henry, a member of a prominent Louisville family, who worked in the same office as Fossey and recognized the girl's shyness. She did not impose. Working together, they became friendly. Soon, Fossey's aloofness began to melt. Mary invited Fossey to her home.

The Henrys were a lively, warm family, and their home was often filled with interesting and unusual guests from all over the world. Fossey was welcomed into their circle and made to feel at home. For the first time in her life, she was part of a caring family, something she had never experienced. Mary's mother, Gaynee Henry, a widow, provided the love and attention that Fossey had not received from her own mother. Still, her newfound friends did not ease the resentment she continued to feel toward her parents.

To her colleagues, Fossey seemed odd in other ways. She lived reclusively, with no neighbors. She found an isolated cottage for rent on a large estate called Glenmary outside the city. Originally used as the laundry building, it had been converted into a small apartment. The estate's owner thought it no place for a single woman, but Fossey threatened to quit her job and leave Louisville if she couldn't live at Glenmary. It took a phone call from someone at the hospital who wanted Fossey to remain for the owner to relent. Fossey immediately loved her new home. "Never

The isolated beauty of Glenmary in autumn captivated Fossey so completely that, once she had seen its little apartment, she refused to live anywhere else. Living alone, caring for animals and surrounded by natural beauty, seems to have suited Fossey's temperament admirably.

have I seen any place as beautiful as this is now in autumn," she wrote in her journal. "The creeks are full of the golden, red, green, and brown leaves from the forests. The pastures are still vivid green and are framed by trees that you would swear were on fire." (Mowat, 3) Before long, the stray dogs and cats in the area learned that scraps of food could always be found around the shabby little cottage. Fossey quickly adopted several of the stray dogs and named them Mitzi, Brownie, and Shep; they became her steadfast companions.

Fossey had no boyfriends, indeed, no social life beyond the Henrys, and she shunned the gossip and small talk among the nurses. Although she loved stylish clothing, she often arrived at the hospital disheveled, with scraggly hair and wrinkled clothing. The Kosair staff left her alone. If they noticed Fossey at all, it was to make fun of her.

Alone in her cottage, Fossey was content. She cooked and baked, took piano lessons, read, and enrolled in a creative-writing course by mail. When Fossey mixed with other tenants around the estate's swimming pool, she occasionally showed a sense of humor, but she was mostly pensive and quiet.

Among the fascinating visitors to the Henry house were Mr. and Mrs. Franz Joseph Forrester, a couple from Rhodesia, in southern Africa, who owned a tobacco farm. Whenever they were guests in the Henry house and Fossey was present, the Forresters invited Fossey and Mary Henry to visit them.

Mary had left her job at the hospital for a position with a travel agency, and her new job enabled her to travel to faraway places. In 1960, when Mary decided to travel to Africa to visit the Forresters, Fossey was envious. Africa's wildlife strongly appealed to her, and when Mary returned with exciting photographs of what she had seen, Fossey was determined to have the same experience. She began to read about African animals, and going on a safari became her primary goal. "I am saving every penny for Africa," Fossey wrote to her mother.

Despite her reticence and unease with others, Fossey secretly yearned for the same things many young women wanted. She recorded her thoughts in a journal that she began at this time. A talented writer, Fossey described her dreams of a meaningful job, of adventure, and of one day having a husband and children. But unlike Mary Henry, Fossey was a 28-year-old single woman with little income and no savings or other resources. The African trip seemed far beyond her reach, a dream to add to her list.

For three more years Fossey led her solitary life of work, accepted as a guest—not quite the same as being one of the family—in the Henry household, a therapist to disabled children, and a protector of stray dogs and cats. Then 31 years old, she felt unfulfilled. Despite her bleak finances, she continued to dream of going on safari. Too stubborn to ask for a loan from her stepfather, Fossey vowed to find another way to see Africa. "Finally," she later wrote, "I realized that dreams seldom materialize on their own." (Matthews, 10)

MATERIALIZING THE DREAM

First, Fossey planned the trip. Although she had as yet no means of funding it, she studied maps, read about the national parks and game preserves, and even took lessons in Swahili, a language widely used in Africa. Her journey's final stop would be a visit with the Henrys' friends, the Forresters, in Rhodesia.

Fossey realized such a trip would require at least seven weeks. She rejected thoughts of packaged tours that planned one's entire itinerary. Rather, she would go alone, hire her own guides, and set her own schedule. She thought of borrowing the money—about $8,000, as much as she earned in 18 months. But with no collateral to offer, Fossey doubted she would obtain such a loan.

Determined to find a lender, though, Fossey trekked from bank to bank until she finally found one willing to lend her the money, though at a very high rate of interest (24%), on the condition that she put up collateral of equal value to hold in the event she failed to repay the money.

In desperation, she finally asked her friend Mary Henry for the required security. Mary immediately put up the collateral, and Fossey mortgaged her income for the next three years to the bank. "I committed myself to a three-year bank debt in order to finance a seven-week safari," she later wrote. (Mowat, 5) But at least she was making it happen.

Fossey read copiously in preparation for her trip. A single work captivated her attention like no other: the American zoologist George Schaller's *The Year of the Gorilla*. Schaller's pioneering studies of Africa's rare mountain gorillas piqued Fossey's imagination and curiosity. Compared to many other primates, little was known about this magnificent species, which had not been discovered by non-native wildlife explorers until 1902.

Fossey's trip required many immunizations against diseases. She had suffered from asthma and allergies throughout her life, and she worried that these would plague her in Africa. Despite her concerns, she got the necessary shots. She bought sturdy boots, insect repellant, and an airplane ticket to Nairobi, the capital of Kenya.

The long, tiring hours of flying, first across the Atlantic, then over Europe, were forgotten at the first glimpse of the vast grasslands of East Africa. From the air, Fossey could see lions and cheetahs, elephants and rhinos, and swift gazelles running in herds. In the rivers, there were water buffaloes, hippopotami, and crocodiles. Always an avid journalist, Fossey noted every aspect of what she was seeing: "Bristly warthogs and baboons everywhere. . . . Buffalo, then rhino, but too dark to photograph. Sykes monkey, Colobus monkey, crested cranes. . . . " (Mowat, 7)

Once in Nairobi, Fossey couldn't wait to get started. She quickly hired an experienced British guide, John Alexander, who knew the land and where to go for the best views of the African wildlife. They would travel a thousand miles in a large circle. The two set out on September 26 to find the gorillas, with Fossey's 44-pound bag of medical supplies in tow.

THE JOURNEY

It wasn't easy. The roads could hardly be called roads; nothing was paved. Rain made them knee-deep in mud. When the land dried, the ruts and holes bounced them up and down on the hard seats of the Land Rover like kids jumping on a trampoline. But Fossey saw everything she had dreamed of: thousands of elephants and rhinos; pink flamingos that hid

THE LEAKEYS: "The First Family of Paleontology"

When Fossey met Louis Leakey, he had already achieved a cult following in the United States; his family has gone on to become synonymous with paleontology, the study of prehistoric life.

Louis S.B. Leakey (1903–1972) was a native of Kenya, born to British missionaries. He was raised in an area in which stone tools could be found accidentally and then studied anthropology at Cambridge. In 1926, he accompanied an expedition to Tanzania—later the land of Jane Goodall's research—as an expert on Africa. He worked in Tanzania to prove Charles Darwin's theory that man's origin was to be found there, and not in Asia as many believed. His first visit to Olduvai Gorge, the site of his most famous discoveries, was in 1931.

He met Mary Douglas Nichols, a fellow anthropologist on a dig in England, and the two worked on the same projects in Tanzania for some time before their marriage. Their son Richard, born in 1944, found his own first fossil at the age of six. He was leading digs by the age of 19, and he became head of the National Museum of Kenya a few years later.

the sky when they took flight; lions and monkeys in trees; hyenas, vultures, zebras, and giraffes in uncountable herds. They climbed to the top of a volcano crater and looked down into a feeding ground where a dozen kinds of animals feasted on the lush plant growth. They crossed flat grasslands that seemed to go on forever in all directions—the Serengeti Plain—and saw hundreds of different species of birds.

Along the way, Alexander suggested a short side trip to Olduvai, the camp of Louis and Mary Leakey at Olduvai

In 1959, searching for the first tool-using humans, the shy and scientifically rigorous Mary found a skull from a genus she called "Zinj" (*Zinjanthropus*). The exhibition of the skull brought the Leakeys fame and, more important, financial support. The couple parted to work independently. Mary continued at Olduvai Gorge, and Louis lectured to raise money. He also launched the work of Jane Goodall with chimpanzees, Dian Fossey with gorillas, and Birute Galdikas with orangutans.

After Louis Leakey's death in 1972, Mary, Richard, and Meave Leakey (Richard's wife, also a paleontologist) continued to make important discoveries and to work toward mapping the complexities of human evolution. In 1978, Mary Leakey discovered the fossilized footprints of a pre-human species, thereby completely altering the model of the evolution of upright walking and suggesting a new species to be added to the evolutionary "family tree." She died in 1996, and now Richard and Meave's daughter Louise has joined the effort. The Leakeys' work has changed, even defined, paleontology, and they will forever be considered its "first family."

Gorge in Tanzania. The Leakeys were the most famous anthropologists in the world. Louis S.B. Leakey had been born in Kenya and had always lived there. His wife, Mary, born in London, had been his student. Together they had found fragments of skulls and bones that were the remains of either humans or species ancestral to humans—some as old as 14 million years—and revolutionized the model of human evolution. Their son, Richard Leakey, would later discover a skull that would lead scientists to believe that human beings lived in Africa about three million years ago.

The Leakeys were accustomed to tourists' being guided to their camp. They did nothing to entertain them, beyond pointing the direction to where they might see some newly found fossils of prehistoric giraffes.

During the visit, Fossey tripped over some rocks in a newly excavated site and sprained her ankle. It began to swell inside her boot. Leakey's staff members carried Fossey back to Olduval, where, she later remembered, they "watched the swelling ankle turn from curious shades of blue to black." Mary Leakey and Alexander concluded that Fossey's plans to climb the Virungas in search of gorillas were now impossible, but they underestimated her resolve. "Neither of them realized that the accident only strengthened my determination to get to the gorillas I had come to meet in Africa," she later wrote. (*Gorillas in the Mist*, 2)

Aided by a walking-stick that a native African had carved for her, Fossey continued her quest. While traveling across the Serengeti, she and her driver met a Belgian man, Jacques Veruschen, who had been the director of Albert National Park, Africa's first wildlife park, in Congo (often called "the Congo"). Fossey told him of her excitement and the many animal species she had seen—but, the Belgian replied, Fossey had seen *nothing* until she had seen the mountain gorillas, the most awesome of all the great apes. Fossey, who had just read Schaller's studies, was eager for an opportunity to see these majestic creatures; Veruschen explained that they were also the most difficult to find, for they were almost extinct. It was believed that only a few hundred existed. And any attempt to see even these would be dangerous. But Fossey didn't care about the dangers or her weak, throbbing ankle. She had made up her mind.

3

The Gorilla Girl: 1963–1966

No one who looks into a gorilla's eyes—intelligent, gentle, vulnerable—can remain unchanged, for the gap between ape and human vanishes; we know that the gorilla still lives within us. Do gorillas also recognize this ancient connection?
—George Schaller, "Gentle Gorillas, Turbulent Times"

THE FIRST ENCOUNTER

In 1963, East Central Africa was in turmoil. New nations were gaining their independence from European rule, but old tribal enemies were using that recently won freedom to kill each other by the hundreds of thousands. No European felt safe in Rwanda, Congo, or Uganda, and the mountains of long-dormant volcanoes called the Virungas—where the mountain gorillas roamed—spanned the borders of all three nations. These mountains had once been at the center of a 20-year disagreement among Belgium, Germany, and

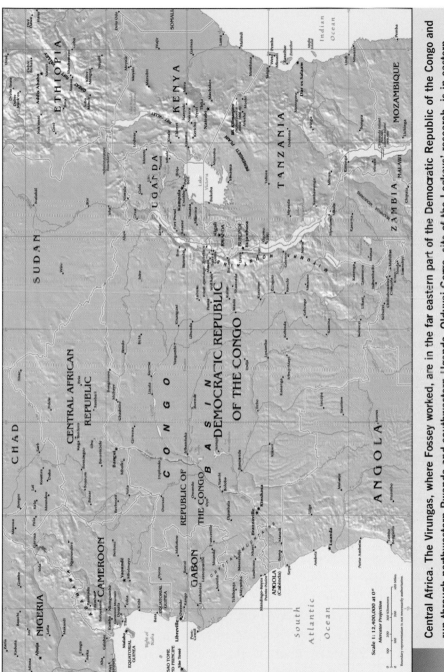

Central Africa. The Virungas, where Fossey worked, are in the far eastern part of the Democratic Republic of the Congo and run through northwestern Rwanda and southwestern Uganda. Olduvai Gorge, site of the Leakeys' research, is in eastern Tanzania, southeast of the Serengeti Plain. In far western Tanzania, almost on the shore of Lake Tanganyika, is Gombe, the home of Jane Goodall's chimpanzees.

Britain. Boundaries had not been established until 1910. At the urging of the American naturalist Carl Akeley, in 1925 Belgium had created Albert National Park; it would be renamed the Parc National des Volcans in 1967.

Jacques Veruschen, the former director of what was then Albert National Park, advised Fossey and her guide that the 14,553-foot Mount Mikeno, on the Congo side of the park, would be the best place to look for gorillas. But first they had to get there. Fossey's driver had never been to the gorilla mountains. He refused to go without first returning to Nairobi to get additional insurance on his Land Rover, in case it was taken away from him. He also wanted a gun to protect them against unfriendly tribesmen or gorillas. He knew nothing about either of them.

Other scientists had studied the elusive primates. In 1960, John Emlen and George Schaller and their wives had camped for six months in the mountains, studying the lowland gorillas and their mountain kin. They managed to get close to the gorillas, sitting and even sleeping among them. They concluded that the magnificent creatures were complex animals with a unique social structure. "My task was not to capture or master them but solely to interpret their life," explained Schaller. "So I approached them with empathy and respect, wanting nothing from them but peace and proximity. And they accepted my presence with an astounding generosity of spirit." (Ake, 2)

Following the Emlens' departure, Schaller stayed on, eventually counting about 400 gorillas. By then the fighting had begun in Congo, and Schaller was forced to flee before his work was complete.

At the inn where they stayed the night before heading into the mountains, Fossey was told to look for a young couple, Alan and Joan Root, world-renowned wildlife photographers who had set up a camp a few weeks earlier to film the gorillas. Alexander and Fossey were nervous as they approached the Congo border. They did not know what to expect from the soldiers who looked them over and studied their passports in silence. The guards finally decided to keep Alexander's passport until he returned. Much to their relief, Alexander and Fossey were then allowed to enter the country.

After an overnight stay at the Albert Park headquarters, they hired 11 porters to carry their equipment. Accompanied by two armed park guards, they began the climb up Mount Mikeno. One of the Congolese park guards, Sanwekwe, was also a skilled tracker who had tracked gorillas as a boy for Carl Akeley and later worked with George Schaller. Sanwekwe would become Fossey's trusted guide.

Fossey's ankle was still tightly bandaged and sore. But she was strong in body and in determination. She was not, however, prepared for what awaited her. The climb was steep, the ground rough, and the growth so thick they never saw the sun overhead. "The terrain was unbelievable, almost straight up," wrote Fossey. "We had to hang on to vines to get along or go on hands and knees." (Matthews, 5)

As they went up, the air thinned. Fossey was soon gasping for breath and had to rest frequently. For over six hours they crept upward along the edges of high cliffs, where one misstep would send them through space into deep canyons. "My rib cage was bursting," Fossey wrote in her journal. "My legs were creaking and in agony, and my ankle felt as though a crocodile had his jaw around it. How those porters do it, each carrying around thirty pounds on his head, I'll never know." (Mowat, 12)

They had reached an altitude of 11,400 feet when they came to a small clearing, where they could see the sun and sky, the mountain peaks, and a camp. The first part of the climb was the steepest, and the thin air had taken its toll on Fossey, a heavy smoker. "You can imagine what happened to my lungs," she wrote later. "It took six and a half hours to get to this camp and I thought I would die."(Mowat, 12) Two surprised young people—Joan and Alan Root—glared at them from the camp. The Roots had not expected tourists and were not pleased to see them; they were there to work, not to entertain visitors.

Fossey and her entourage pitched tents for the night. The next day, with no help from the Roots, who wished to be rid of them, they wandered about the mountains on their own and saw nothing. Still, Fossey was determined not to leave until she saw the gorillas. For the next few days she tried to make friends with the Roots, inviting them to tea at her tent. She told them how she loved animals and would be sorely disappointed if, after traveling this far, she had to leave without seeing the rare mountain gorillas. The Roots at last agreed to take her with them the next day.

The first thing Fossey noticed as they hacked their way through the thick jungle growth was an odor that reminded her of a farm and men working, sweating in the sun. Then she heard a screaming sound unlike any she had ever heard. One of the trackers swung his machet and cut a hole in the bush. The space was suddenly filled by the massive, staring head of a gigantic gorilla. Fossey stared at her ancestral past and her future. She recalled the encounter in *Gorillas in the Mist*:

> Sound preceded sight. Odor preceded sound in the form of an overwhelming musky-barnyard, human-like scent. The air was suddenly rent by a high-pitched series of screams followed by the rhythmic rondo of sharp pok-pok chest beats from a great silverback male obscured behind what seemed an impenetrable wall of vegetation. . . . The three of us froze until the echoes of the screams and chest beats faded. . . . Peeking through the vegetation, we could distinguish

Fossey's first encounter with the gorillas strengthened her resolve to return. "Peeking through the vegetation, we could distinguish an equally curious phalanx of black, leather-countenanced, furry-headed primates peering back at us," she wrote. "Their bright eyes darted nervously from under heavy brows as though trying to identify us as familiar friends or possible foes."

an equally curious phalanx of black, leather-countenanced, furry-headed primates peering back at us.
Their bright eyes darted nervously from under heavy
brows as though trying to identify us as familiar
friends or possible foes. Immediately I was struck by
the physical magnificence of the huge jet-black bodies
blended against the green palette wash of the thick
forest foliage.

(3)

Fossey's description of the initial encounter testifies to
the eye for detail, and the Goodall-like tendency to think of
the subjects almost as humans, that served her so well in
her research:

A group of about six adult gorillas stared apprehen-
sively back at us through the opening in the wall of
vegetation. A phalanx of enormous, half-seen, looming
black bodies surmounted by shiny black patent-leather
faces with deep-set warm brown eyes. They were big
and imposing, but not monstrous at all. Somehow they
looked more like members of a picnic party surprised
by interlopers.

(Mowat, 14)

Fossey's cook, Manuel, also was seeing his first gorilla.
"*Kweli nudugu yanga,*" he whispered in Swahili—"Surely,
God, these are my kin." (Mowat, 14) Fossey had to leave
Mount Mikeno soon afterward, but she was determined not
to have seen her last gorilla.

Because Fossey was so often at odds with the people
around her, one more episode that took place before her
return to America is worth mentioning: a brief love affair.
She stopped in Rhodesia to visit the Forrester family,
whom she had met at Mary Henry's home in Louisville.
Delighted to see her, the Forresters welcomed her to their

farm. They introduced her to their stocky, six-foot-two son, Alexie, who was about to begin college at the University of Notre Dame in Indiana. Alexie was quickly impressed by Fossey, who, with characteristic enthusiasm, eagerly climbed onto a tractor and volunteered to plow a field. The two fell in love during the visit and talked of marriage. But Alexie wanted to graduate from college first, and Fossey didn't want to wait that long. The relationship did not survive.

Despite this unexpected turmoil before her departure, one truth still existed for Fossey when she boarded the plane to the United States. She knew she'd return to Africa. "I left Kabara with reluctance but with never a doubt that I would, somehow, return to learn more about the gorillas of the misted mountains." (*Gorillas in the Mist*, 4)

"I WOULD, SOMEHOW, RETURN"

When Fossey returned to Kosair Children's Hospital in Louisville in November of 1963, she sent articles about her trip to major magazines and journals All were rejected. She also submitted a manuscript for a book for young people about her trip and the gorillas to the publishing company Doubleday in New York. But Doubleday recommended that her book be rewritten for adults, who would better appreciate the wealth of information Fossey had collected. Only the Louisville newspapers published her stories.

Frustrated by these rejections, Fossey still faced the enormous task of repaying the $8,000 loan for her trip to Africa. For the next two years, more than half of each paycheck she earned went to paying her debts, forcing her to cut expenses. When Fossey's treasured privacy was diminished by a mobile home parked near her shack, she moved to an even more isolated location, one with no heat or running water. While she lived in these conditions, Fossey's health deteriorated. In the spring of 1966, she contracted

Louis Leakey studied humans through studying other primates. He was the force behind the revolutionary work of Dian Fossey, Jane Goodall, and Birute Galdikas; all three broke new ground in their research, and Goodall and Galdikas continue their work to this day. Fossey was thrilled to become his "gorilla girl."

an infection that resulted in a painful series of boils. Burdened with debts, though, Fossey refused to take any time off from work.

During this difficult time, a doctor at Kosair Hospital asked Fossey whether she was aware that Louis Leakey, the famous paleoanthropologist she had met briefly during her trip to Africa, would be lecturing at the University of Louisville on Sunday evening, April 3. Leakey's fame had grown in recent years with the expansion of his work. He was constantly engaged in projects: breeding monkeys, directing an array of studies from ancient bones to living primates, and supervising digs in Africa, Israel, and the United States.

Leakey believed that long-term studies of the great apes would shed light on human evolution. Fossey was intrigued by Leakey's theories about the connections between primate and human behavior. "From them we may learn much concerning the behavior of our earliest primate prototypes," Fossey later explained, "because behavior, unlike bones, teeth, or tools, does not fossilize." (*Gorillas in the Mist*, xvi) Initially, Leakey had focused on chimpanzees, which are genetically close to humans. He had initiated the long-term study of chimpanzees that had thrust Jane Goodall into the international spotlight in 1960. He also hoped to find the means to begin similar studies of orangutans and mountain gorillas, but this would require constant fundraising, so he toured and lectured frequently to stimulate public interest.

When Leakey addressed the audience in a lecture hall in Louisville on the night of April 3, Fossey listened eagerly. In her hands she held copies of the newspaper articles she had written, illustrated with photographs given to her by the Roots.

After Leakey's talk, Fossey stood in a long line of admirers waiting to speak with him. When she reached Leakey, he immediately recognized her. "Miss Fossey, isn't it?" he asked.

"Please wait until I've finished with all these people." Finally, the crowd dwindled, and he addressed Fossey. He was indifferent to the articles she handed him until he saw the pictures of the gorillas. "I told him that I wanted to spend my life working with animals—that had always been my dream," she later remembered. "And that I was especially interested in the gorillas on the Virunga mountains." "And how is your ankle?" asked Leakey, unexpectedly. "Did it heal properly?" Fossey couldn't believe that Leakey remembered her at all, and what he said next astonished her: "Come to my hotel tomorrow morning at eight. You might be just the person I have in mind to start a long-term study of gorillas." (Mowat, 21, 22)

BECOMING THE GORILLA GIRL

The next morning, Leakey interviewed Fossey for over an hour. He praised Jane Goodall, who had been doing her pioneering work with African chimpanzees for six years, and told Fossey of his intention to employ someone to conduct similar studies on gorillas. Although Dr. Leakey had interviewed 22 applicants to work with the gorillas, he expressed his belief that Fossey was an ideal candidate. She had no scientific background, but that didn't matter; he wasn't interested in statistics as much as behavioral patterns. Leakey realized that women were more sensitive to the interactions of mothers and infants, males and females, and rival group leaders, which did not require scientific training to observe. "I have no use for overtrained people," Fossey remembered Leakey saying. "I prefer those who are not specifically educated for this field since they go into the work with open minds and without prejudice and preconceptions." (Mowat, 22)

In Leakey's words, Fossey would become "the gorilla girl." But before such a study began he had to acquire the necessary funding. He ended their conversation by advising Fossey to have her appendix removed if she intended to return to Africa, explaining that an attack of appendicitis could prove fatal if one lived in a remote area where medical treatment was miles away. Fossey immediately made plans for the surgery.

Six weeks after Fossey's appendectomy in the summer of 1966, she received a letter from Dr. Leakey. Its opening lines introduced her to what she came to know as his unique sense of humor. "Actually, there really isn't a dire need for you to have your appendix removed," he wrote. "That is only my way of testing applicants' determination!" (*Gorillas in the Mist*, 4)

Having worked for two years to pay off her debts, Fossey resigned from her position at Kosair. She headed to California to visit her parents while awaiting the news that Dr. Leakey had obtained funding for the gorilla study. Although she was excited about the next phase of her life, she also found it difficult to leave Louisville: "Now it was time to take the next step toward Kabara, which meant severing the deep attachments of many years in Louisville. Leaving the place I'd grown to love— the children, my home, the farm dogs, and my friends—was one of the most difficult things I'd ever had to do." (Mowat, 24)

For Fossey, the greatest hardship was leaving her dogs, Mitzi, Brownie, and Shep. It seemed that they understood she would not return. "There was no way that I could explain to dogs, friends, or parents my compelling need to return to Africa to launch a long-term study of the gorillas," she later explained. "Some may call it destiny and others may call it dismaying. I call the sudden turn of events in my life fortuitous." (*Gorillas in the Mist*, 5)

Kitty Price was dismayed by her daughter's plans and questioned the wisdom of the venture. "Why can't you be like other girls?" she asked. "Look at Mary Henry, how happy she is. What have you done with your real opportunities?" With characteristic confidence, Fossey replied, "I'm different from Mary. I want different things." (Mowat, 24)

As Fossey waited in California, months passed with no word from Dr. Leakey. In December she finally received word that the gorilla project would be funded with $3,000 from Leighton Wilkie, who had also funded Jane Goodall's long-term chimpanzee study. Wilkie shared Leakey's belief that human evolution could best be understood through a greater knowledge of man's closest relatives. On December 19, Fossey departed for Africa, a copy of *Teach Yourself Swahili* tucked under her arm.

At 34, Fossey had finally attained a personal vision.

BECOME A PRIMATOLOGIST

Primatologists, researchers devoted to the study of primates, represent a diverse group of conservationists, scientists, educators, veterinarians, and medical researchers. Many educational paths can make this career a possibility. The American Society of Primatologists reports that most who enter the field have backgrounds in biology/zoology, psychology, anthropology, or veterinary science. The most appropriate courses of undergraduate training, though, are those in science education, ecology and conservation, biology, journalism or scientific writing, molecular biology, animal behavior, virology, paleontology, geology, natural-resource management, or even statistics and computer science. Advanced degrees may be required, depending on the type of position the candidate wishes to find, from universities offering courses in those fields or from medical or veterinary schools. Most important are a background in biology and excellent communication skills. A knowledge of statistics helps, too, in research like Dr. Fossey's. A love of, and respect for, the animals is essential.

Her life's purpose was clear. "I had a deep wish to see and live with wild animals in a world that hadn't been yet completely changed by humans," she wrote. "I guess I really wanted to go backward in time. . . . The thought of being where the animals haven't all been driven into little corners attracts me so much." (Matthews, 5)

4

Kabara: 1966–1967

A ROCKY START

When Fossey arrived in Nairobi, just before Christmas of 1966, her head aching with a cold and fever, she had no idea what challenges awaited her. She knew nothing about the rain forests, the oozing, waist-deep mud, the unending wetness, the customs and attitudes of the Africans she would have to rely on to guide her and work for her, the languages (some countries had hundreds of dialects), or the loneliness that grew as heavy as the plant life. No one really understood what was happening politically in the newly independent countries of Congo, Uganda, and Rwanda. Caucasian Europeans fleeing to safety told of soldiers and bandits slaughtering thousands of all ethnicities, for little or no reason.

However, as Fossey's plane touched down in Africa, her mind wasn't attuned to the turmoil within its boundaries. Instead, her thoughts were filled with George Schaller's earlier

Fossey logged thousands of hours in the bush, patiently recording the behavior of mountain gorillas like this silverback. When the gorillas would not allow her to get close enough to photograph them, she sketched their nose prints. She had her trusted guide, Sanwekwe, to thank for much of her early instruction in navigating the rain forest.

findings. Thanks to Schaller, who had spent some 458 hours observing the gorillas in 1960, Fossey knew more about the mountain gorillas she intended to study for the next two years than anything else about her new life. While in California before her departure for Africa, Fossey had reread Schaller's works, *The Mountain Gorilla: Ecology and Behavior*, *The Year of the Gorilla*, and *Primate Behavior*.

The 400-pound silverbacks, so called because their coats turn gray across their backs as they grow older, dominate each family or group. The gorillas spend most of every day eating over 200 types of leaves, fruit, fungi, tubers, and flowers, including wild celery, bamboo, thistles, and bracket fungus, a hard, shell-like fungus that grows on tree trunks. Occasionally, they consume insects, such as termites. Unlike chimpanzees, they do not hunt or eat meat. They get enough moisture from the large quantities of foliage they consume, and they usually avoid bodies of water. It was once believed that gorillas never drank water, but more recent studies have observed them occasionally drinking it—even frolicking in it, as humans tend to do. Each day, they gather branches and build new nests for the night, sleeping through approximately 13 of every 24 hours. The females care for the young. In times of danger, the males rise up, thump their chests with their huge paws, shriek, and rush their attackers. Hunters seeking baby gorillas for sale to zoos around the world have had to fight the silverback guardians to the death.

It soon became obvious to others that while Fossey felt she knew much about the gorillas she had come to study, she understood almost nothing about Africa's political turmoil and the dangers of traveling and living alone there. When Fossey changed planes in a London airport, she had the very good fortune to run into Joan Root, who with her husband had befriended Fossey during the first trip to Africa in 1963. As Root listened to Fossey's plans, she was amazed to learn that Dr. Leakey had suggested that Fossey drive the 700 miles from Nairobi to Congo alone.

After the two women talked further, Root realized that Fossey lacked the knowledge required to live alone in such a remote region of Africa. She also saw that Fossey wasn't well. Realizing that Fossey's plans were foolhardy, Root insisted that

George B. Schaller, shown in 1993. His work with mountain gorillas preceded Fossey's, and she was fascinated by his *The Year of the Gorilla* even before her first sight of Africa. "I approached them with empathy and respect," Schaller said of his work with the gorillas, "wanting nothing from them but peace and proximity. And they accepted my presence with an astounding generosity of spirit."

her husband accompany Fossey in his Land Rover on the long journey to Congo. As an experienced camper familiar with the mountainous climate and environment, She helped Fossey to shop for the equipment and camp supplies she would need.

Dr. Leakey met Fossey in Nairobi and set out to find her a suitable vehicle for the grueling journey she was about to undertake. Fossey reported, "Dr. Leakey purchased, after some perilous test drives through Nairobi's crowded streets, an antiquated, canvas-topped Land Rover that I later named 'Lily.'" (*Gorillas in the Mist*, 5) One of the natives who worked for Dr. Leakey gave Fossey driving lessons. But he spoke only Swahili, so as he gave her directions she had to thumb through a Swahili–English dictionary. He also frequently yelled at Fossey in Swahili, but this she somehow understood.

Before departing for Congo, Fossey visited Jane Goodall's camp at the Gombe Stream Research Centre. Dr. Leakey had arranged for her to spend Christmas with Goodall, hoping that Fossey could learn much from Goodall's experience in setting up a research camp in the rain forest. But Fossey seemed far too idealistic to the veteran Goodall. In a letter to her mother, written in mid-January of 1967, Goodall referred to Fossey as "the gorilla girl" and expressed some skepticism about Leakey's new researcher:

> She seems to have the most romantic ideas in her head. She keeps saying the meadow is like an alpine meadow. She is determined to get a cow up there, and lots of hens. She will have a bell around the cow's neck. . . . She plans to make bramble jam out of the wild blackberries. Well, when I began with the chimps, I had romantic notions, too. . . . Next we found out that she had not even read [Schaller's] book carefully. Nor has she during the past three years since she planned to study gorillas, bothered to learn anything about primates. . . . However, let us hope for the best.

(Goodall, *Beyond Innocence*, 31–32)

Finally, on December 31, Fossey and Alan Root headed for Congo. Root drove his Land Rover just ahead of Fossey, over rutted, crater-filled roads. Driving at night was out of the question; one could easily slide into a mudhole or drop a thousand feet off the edge of the road. Once, one of Fossey's wheels actually fell off, and without Root she would have been lost. Root fearlessly talked their way past border crossings and police barriers.

THE ARRIVAL AT KABARA

On the morning of January 6, 1967, Fossey and Root, accompanied by some Congolese park guards and two natives who had agreed to work for Fossey, arrived at Kabara, a village at the foot of Mount Mikeno. Sanwekwe, the trusted guide she had met during her first trip to Africa, would join the camp's staff later. Just as she had done in 1963, Fossey hired porters—this time, several dozen—to cart her supplies and equipment to the plateau, located nearly four 4,000 feet above. Climbing the mountain was arduous. The air was damp and cold, but the exertion of the ascent made the climbers sweat profusely. Fossey, a heavy smoker, struggled to breathe in the thin air. At last they reached the plateau on which Fossey had camped in 1963. She was pleased to find that little had changed in the three years since she had left the lush, green meadow.

Root spent the next two days helping Fossey to establish her camp. He supervised the digging of the drainage ditches around the tents and the latrine, which was draped with potato-sack curtain. When Root left her on January 15, Fossey suddenly realized that she was now the only English-speaking person on the mountain. Later, she described her terror as Root began his descent down the mountain: "I clung on to my tent pole simply to avoid running after him." (*Gorillas in the Mist*, 7)

The following day was Fossey's 35th birthday. She now shared the camp with two native Africans with whom she could not converse. The humid air carried soft sounds of insects and occasional squeals and screams as Fossey lay in her 7'-by-10' tent, her home and office for the next two years. The crude pavilion was decorated with bright-colored native fabric draped over wooden crates that served as cupboards, filing cabinets, desks, and chairs.

During that first day alone with the native guards, one them approached her tent and asked, in Swahili, "*Unapenda maji moto?*" At first, Fossey misunderstood and thought he was threatening her. She began to cry and zipped herself into her tent. After an hour or so, her doubts subsided, and she asked the African to repeat his question slowly. He had merely asked if she wanted some hot water. She managed at last to thank him: "I accepted a couple of gallons of hot water as graciously as possible with many *asantes*." (*Gorillas in the Mist*, 7)

Fossey was encouraged when Dr. Leakey wrote that he hoped to obtain additional funding for the gorillas project from the National Geographic Society. The Society's funding was important, but its support also would guarantee films, articles, and lecture tours. Fossey and Dr. Leakey hoped that the media exposure would generate interest in conserving the dwindling gorilla population.

Sanwekwe's presence, too, was comforting, helping to alleviate a menacing cloud of suspicion that hung over the camp. Fossey believed the two other native staff members were stealing from her. Sometimes the guards didn't appear in camp for days. They also talked among themselves in their native language, Kinyarwanda, a language that relies on verbal inflection and body language. Because Fossey couldn't understand what they were saying, her suspicions grew. When she went down to the park headquarters, where she kept her Land Rover, she usually found the guards drunk. She also discovered that her Land Rover had been driven but that no one would tell her by whom. These incidents fed Fossey's growing disenchantment with native Africans.

Sanwekwe brought a welcome-gift to the camp, a rooster and a hen whom Fossey named Desi and Lucy. Their eggs were a vast improvement over the camp's staples of corn, sweet and white potatoes, and beans. While the natives preferred those foods, Fossey preferred canned items— sausages, hash, tuna, Spam, and corned beef. She supplemented these with noodles, oatmeal, spaghetti, and sweets, such as Oreo cookies. When food supplies ran low, Fossey survived on potatoes. Meals were cooked and eaten in the men's hut, a small, aging wooden structure. The natives cooked their own food on a fire in the middle of the smoky room they occupied.

Fossey made monthly trips to Kisoro, Uganda, a two-hour drive from the base of Mount Mikeno, to buy a two week supply of fresh foods, cheese, and bread. "A month thus tended to be divided into two parts," she wrote. "Feast for the first half and fast throughout the remaining days." (*Gorillas in the Mist*, 9)

One of the greatest hardships Fossey endured was an occasional lack of cigarettes. A chain-smoker, she would limit herself to several puffs on a few remaining cigarettes until a new supply was obtained in Kisoro. Fossey and Sanwekwe often joked about their shared addiction. The tracker smoked a pipe and often stretched his own tobacco supply by blending it with dry leaves.

Fossey's relationship with Sanwekwe grew stronger during their first months of fieldwork, searching for and observing gorillas. She depended on him for her very life. He kept her from becoming hopelessly lost when they walked for hours through pouring rain, and taught her how to position herself to observe the gorillas without disturbing them.

During her first outing, she hadn't walked more than ten minutes from camp when she saw a lone male gorilla sunbathing on a log in an open area near a small lake. Startled by Fossey's presence, it vanished into the forest. But in another gorilla encounter, the males did not flee. Fossey described the terrifying incident in her journal:

> Today Sanwekwe and I were charged by two gorillas, and it wasn't a bluff charge—they really meant it. We were about one hundred and fifty feet directly downhill from a group when a silverback and a female decided to eradicate us. They gave us a split second of warning and screams and roars that seemed to come from every direction at once before they descended in a gallop that shook the ground. I was determined to stand fast, but when they broke through the foliage at a dead run directly above me, I felt my legs retreating in spite of what I've read about gorillas not charging fully. I paused long enough to try to dissuade them with my voice, which only seemed to aggravate them more, if possible; and when their long, yellow canines and wild eyes were no less than two feet away, I took a very ungainly nosedive into the thick foliage alongside the trail.
>
> (Mowat, 33)

Fortunately, however, Fossey and her devoted guide managed to outmaneuver the ungainly gorillas, at the expense of considerable discomfort:

> They whizzed on by, caught up in their own momentum. It's a good thing they didn't come back to attack, for I was certainly in no position to defend myself. It may have taken only a split second to dive into that foliage, but it took about fifteen minutes to extract myself—what a tangle!
>
> (Mowat, 33)

ACCEPTING THE ANIMALS ON THEIR OWN TERMS

The gorillas lived in groups whose composition changed according to births, deaths, and the movements of individual gorillas. A sexually mature male silverback, over 15 years old, weighing about 375 pounds, led each group. A group also contained one blackback, a younger, sexually immature male, whose age might be 8 to 13 years, and several sexually mature females averaging 8 years or older and weighing approximately 200 pounds. Under normal conditions, these females were mated to the dominant silverback for life. The other group members included immature gorillas, usually under the age of 8 and classified according to age and weight as young adults, juveniles, or infants.

Every evening, the groups made nests of leaves and twigs, usually on the ground. In the morning, led by the silverback, they began roaming, feeding along the way. At about 10:00 A.M. they would stop to rest for two to four hours, sleeping in newly made nests. The adults were very tolerant of and gentle with the young, allowing them to pull on their hair, slide down their backs, romp around them, or cuddle close beside them. Following the morning rest, they would resume wandering and feeding until dusk, then gather foliage to make a nest and retire for the night.

Fossey and Sanwekwe adopted a regimen of long days that began at 5:30 A.M. and evenings occupied by numerous camp chores. Fossey devoted nights to typing her detailed notes on her portable typewriter about every aspect of life on the mountain and her contact with the gorillas. When time allowed, Fossey also recorded her observations about plants and wildlife, the weather, and poachers. She carefully sent copies of all her notes to Dr. Leakey, eagerly sharing each detail with him. "It was always a most delightful, cozy feeling," she wrote, "to type up field notes near the crackling fireplace at night with the sounds of the owls, hyrax, antelope, buffalo, and elephants outside." (Matthews, 28)

Initially, Fossey's attempts to observe gorilla groups were unsuccessful. Unaccustomed to her presence, the gorillas would flee into the forest when she appeared. Patiently, Fossey learned that she would have to remain concealed, watching the gorillas

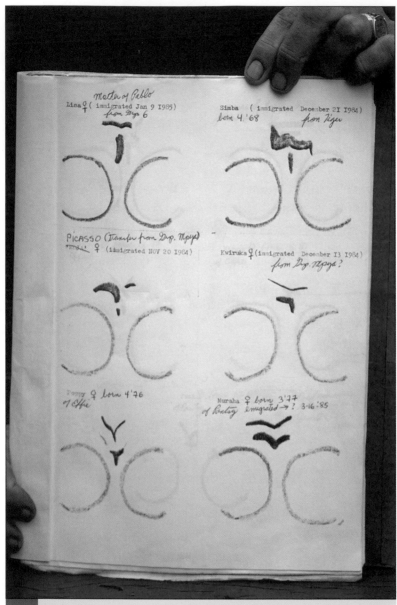

This is one of Fossey's record books, showing the nose prints of six of the gorillas she was studying. The print on the upper right is that of Simba, the mate of one of Fossey's favorite gorillas, Digit.

through binoculars, before she could make open contact with them. That was the only way she could learn their behavior without scaring them away. Eventually, Fossey realized that to be accepted required a familiarity with every detail of their existence: their daily habits, their vocalizations, their gestures, their individual identities.

More than seven years before the start of Fossey's field research, George Schaller had coined the term *nose prints* to describe his method of identifying the individuals within each group. Fossey explained, "As no two humans have exactly the same fingerprints, no two gorillas have the same nose print—the shape of the nostrils and the outstanding troughs seen on the bridges of their noses." (*Gorillas in the Mist,* 11) Unable to get close enough to photograph them, she drew sketches of the gorillas' nose prints.

Fossey gradually gained confidence with each challenge that confronted her. After months spent mastering the ability to use binoculars while taking notes and sketching, she began taking photographs on sunny days. As the gorillas came to accept her presence, she would climb a tree and capture magnificent shots of groups of gorillas who had watched her struggle to climb the tree, an activity they performed easily. Fossey realized the importance of mimicking gorilla behavior.

One idea led to another. Fossey suspected that standing might be a human posture that frightened gorillas, so she began to crawl, calling this "the beginning of my knuckle-walking days." She learned to mimic or "ape" their eating habits and chomp upon wild celery just as they did. Fossey explained, "I therefore changed my tactics from climbing trees to view the gorillas to leaving the trees for the gorillas to climb to view me. . . . The Kabara group taught me much regarding gorilla behavior. From them I learned to accept the animals on their own terms." (Fossey, 14)

Gorillas have no enemies among other animals, only humans. Mountain gorillas are gentle, nonviolent except when

GORILLA GORILLA

Taxonomy is the system that scientists use to make sense of the many life forms that live or have lived in the Earth's biosphere. Living things are grouped into *taxa* (sing. *taxon*), categories that can include millions of creatures or only one. Grouping is first by kingdom (there are five) and then by, in decreasing order of size, *phylum* (pl. *phyla*) or *division*; *class*; *order* or *subclass*; *family*; *genus* (pl. *genera*); and *species*. (Subcategories are added when necessary to describe evolutionary distinctions, and there *is* some variation in the system.) The more closely interrelated two beings are, the more classifications they will have in common. Humans and gorillas both are primates; the two species are of the same kingdom, phylum, subphylum, class, and order but diverge at the family level. Gorillas (*Gorilla gorilla*) are classified as follows:

Kingdom	*Animalia* (all animals) or *Metazoa* (all organisms composed of multiple cells)
Phylum	*Chordata* (all animals that express certain developmental characteristics)
Subphylum	*Vertebrata* (all chordates that develop a backbone)
Class	*Mammalia* (all warm-blooded vertebrates, fur, mammary glands, and live birth)
Order	*Primata* (11 families, including the great apes and humans)
Family	*Pongidae* (all great apes, including gorillas, chimpanzees, bonobos, and orangutans)
Genus	*Gorilla* (gorillas and orangutans)
Species	*gorilla* (gorillas only)
Subspecies	*graueri* (the eastern lowland gorilla)
Subspecies	*beringei* (the mountain gorilla, found in Rwanda and Uganda)
Subspecies	*gorilla* (the western lowland gorilla, the subspecies found in Congo)

threatened, but then they will fight fiercely. If any group member is attacked, the adults will fight to the death in defense; many males had died in doing this to protect infants from poachers. Fossey quickly developed a profound hatred for the poachers, who were primarily Pygmy tribesmen. In March of 1967, she and Sanwekwe attempted to locate gorillas at a lower altitude on the volcano mountain. They found it filled with Pygmy tribal hunters known as Twa, and Fossey confronted four of them. "We met them in the deepest, darkest part of the forest, and while Sanwekwe held the gun on them I took their spears and pangas. . . . That was easily the most horrible day of my life." (Mowat, 35) She also believed, "If I can enforce the written rules of a supposedly protected park against the slaughter of animals, then I must do it." (Matthews, 31)

Although Fossey seemed fearless, she was filled with nagging doubts and uncertainties. Difficulties with her native staff continued. At times Fossey described her mood as "black." Her dark mood surely would have deepened if she had known of the escalating political turmoil that engulfed the nation of Congo. But, aside from the mail she received from Dr. Leakey and her American friends, Fossey was completely isolated from news. Her correspondence with Leakey reflects her view of the time: "I don't like writing the following any more than you're going to enjoy reading it, but the fact remains that I must have some 'help' up here as soon as possible, if only for a few weeks." (Mowat, 38)

5

Political Turmoil, New Friends, and Rwanda: 1967–1968

FOSSEY IN PRISON

In July of 1967, fighting broke out among factions of the Congolese army in the cities surrounding the Albert National Park. The Congolese president, Mobutu Sese Seko, had hired white mercenary soldiers, well-paid and more reliable than his regular soldiers, and put them in command of his native army. On July 5, though, the white officers turned against the president and the rest of the Congolese soldiers. Overnight, cities and towns became battlegrounds. The borders were closed. Disorder and destruction permeated the area. All white people, Mobutu announced, were now to be considered the enemy—and should be killed.

Fossey knew nothing of this until she returned from her observations on the afternoon of July 9. Thirty park guards and porters were waiting for her. They had orders to dismantle her camp and take her and all her possessions

Fossey standing before Karisoke. Alyette de Munck financed the first building, consisting of two rooms, in 1968, replacing the three small, ramshackle tents from which Fossey had been operating for about a year. The area has not always been friendly to the efforts of anthropologists, though, and the camp has always been far from secure.

down the mountain to the town of Rumamgbo—all for her protection, they said. "I have to admit I spent a great deal of time in tears, especially when the mats were stripped from the walls of the hut, my tent was taken down, and all the work I'd done for the past six months was undone," Fossey later wrote. "I never fully realized what that place meant to me until I had to give it up, not knowing if I would be able to return or not." (Mowat, 41)

Fossey protested but had no choice. She was taken to a farmhouse and left there, in comfort but uncertain over her fate. She managed to get a letter out to Dr. Leakey telling him of her whereabouts. Some civilian airplanes had been shot down, but Leakey sent a plane to rescue Fossey. The pilot was unable to find her.

It remains unclear what kind of ordeal Dian Fossey endured for 16 days before she escaped. Her own accounts varied in the telling. She talked of being left in a cage for two days, and of natives' yelling and spitting at her. There may have been several white men in the cage with her; she said they were all murdered. She was undoubtedly harassed but later appeared to have suffered no physical harm. One day, she persuaded her guards that she needed money to pay them. They accompanied her across the nearby border into Uganda to get it and make sure she returned. A few days later, determined to escape, she again told the guards she needed money. To avoid suspicion she left most of her belongings behind, taking only her notes, her typewriter, and her rooster and hen. As before, a soldier rode with her in the Land Rover. At the border, Fossey bribed the guards to let them through. When they arrived at the inn at which she had stayed before her first trek up the mountain, Fossey fled and hid.

The innkeeper, a European named Walter Baumgartel, protected her. Ignoring a pursuing guard's plea that his commander would shoot him if he returned without Fossey, Baumgartel called Ugandan soldiers and had them escort the guard back to the Congo border, to whatever fate awaited.

Safe for the moment, Fossey turned all her determination to returning to her gorillas. She could never go back to Congo,

Declaring that white people were the enemy, the Congolese president, Mobutu Sese Seko, ordered the dismantling of Fossey's camp in July of 1967. "I never fully realized what that place meant to me," she wrote, "until I had to give it up, not knowing if I would be able to return or not."

but there were parts of the park in Rwanda and Uganda, and the borders meant nothing to the mountain gorillas. Fossey was certain of one thing: she was not going back to the U.S. She would have to find a way to return to the Virungas.

ROSAMOND HALSEY CARR AND ALYETTE DE MUNCK

Rosamond Halsey Carr, an American expatriate and owner of a plantation in Rwanda, was lunching at the home of the American military attaché in Kigali when she first met Dian Fossey, in late July of that year. Carr, who had grown up in New Jersey, had gone to Africa in 1949 after marrying an older man who owned a coffee plantation and gold and tin mines. She had later divorced him and then remained in Africa, living alone on a plantation near the base of Mount Karisimbi, where she grew flowers to supply the area's resort hotels.

Carr knew of Fossey's work at Kabara. Weeks earlier, Kitty Cyr, the wife of the United States ambassador, Leo Cyr, had learned that Fossey hoped to reestablish her camp on Carr's plantation. Kitty Cyr warned Carr of Fossey's plans, "Roz, there's a young woman who has been studying the mountain gorillas in the Congo. You be careful. She's a strange one." (Carr, 154)

Carr recalled her introduction to Fossey. "The moment I arrived, I was accosted by an exceptionally tall young woman dressed in a lovely lilac linen dress and filthy tennis shoes," Carr later wrote. "Her dark hair was worn in a thick braid over one shoulder, and her brown eyes were startling in their scrutiny. She conveyed in her demeanor no sense of friendliness or charm whatsoever, but rather a steely determination." (Carr, 156) Only later did Carr learn that Fossey wore the same shoes that she'd had on when forced down the mountain. She had no others.

"Now, Mrs. Carr," Fossey began, "I have some questions to ask you." And then she rattled off: "Question one—," "Question two—," "Question three—." Carr told Fossey that there were no gorillas on her side of the mountain; Fossey retorted, "I know they are there."

Carr agreed to allow Fossey to set up temporary quarters on her plantation. Gradually the two women developed a lasting friendship. Carr, a strong, independent woman, understood better than anyone the importance of female friends to non-native women living in Africa. Such women endured loneliness and isolation, and friendships proved vital to their survival in a strange culture and an often dangerous environment.

Carr also introduced Fossey to a Belgian friend, Alyette de Munck. De Munck, 45, a naturalist and explorer in her own right, had lived in Africa most of her life. She and her husband, Adrien de Munck, a mining engineer, had raised a son and a nephew in Congo. De Munck knew every Pygmy, every volcano, and all the flora and fauna of central Africa. When the fighting broke out, they had sent the boys to school in Belgium. Forced to leave their home, they had moved to Rwanda, to a plantation near Rosamond Carr's.

The de Muncks had returned to Europe in May, and Adrien had died suddenly of a heart attack in Paris on June 6. Not only did Carr believe that de Munck and Fossey had much in common, she felt that helping Fossey would be just the challenge de Munck needed to help ease the profound grief over her husband's death. Carr told Fossey that on August 6 de Munck would fly into Nairobi, where she would meet her son and nephew who were returning from a safari. Carr suggested that Fossey meet de Munck in Nairobi.

Fossey liked Carr's idea. She needed to confer with Dr. Leakey at his home in Nairobi and she was eager to meet de Munck. When Fossey arrived in the city on August 1, Dr. Leakey greeted her with good news. Fossey's work had impressed her sponsors at the National Geographic Society and brought in more money for her to continue her field studies. She would now be under their exclusive sponsorship and would write articles for their magazine and help in the filming of documentaries for television. The financing did not include a salary; she never earned a salary, in all her years in Africa, and money would always be in short supply for her. But getting back to her gorillas was all that mattered.

Fossey was at the Nairobi airport on August 6 when Alyette de Munck arrived and was met by her son and nephew and one of their friends. When Fossey explained her purpose in being there and asked for their aid, they all immediately agreed to help her find her gorillas. The de Munck family began the long drive in their jeep; Fossey would fly to Nagali a week later where de Munck and the boys would be waiting for her.

Fossey busied herself loading up on supplies for her new camp. One day she received a cable from the American Embassy in Kigali informing her that everyone who had escaped from Congo must now leave Rwanda. If they refused, they could be turned over to the Congolese they had fled. Fossey read it, tore it up, and headed for Rwanda.

UNITED IN SORROW

Rwanda is a tiny landlocked country in east central Africa about the size of the state of Maryland. At the time Fossey arrived there, it had been an independent country for five years. Ignored by developers and colonizers for centuries, it was the most crowded, impoverished country on the continent. Despite off-and-on wars between the two principal tribes, white families living there had not been threatened.

The greatest danger was to the land itself. The population was over three million and growing. There was never enough food. Trees were cut, jungle growth cleared almost to extinction to clear more and more land to grow crops. The few livestock were constantly searching for new grazing land. This spread of farms and people and grazing animals inevitably reached the national parks on the slopes of the Virunga volcanoes. The land preserved for wildlife, including gorillas, had been steadily shrinking, and was frequently invaded by herds of cattle and families of squatters.

The gorillas were also threatened by poachers, who captured gorilla infants to sell to zoos and killed adult gorillas for their paws and heads, which brought high prices on the black market. The heads and paws were used for potions and talismans for native consumers. Fossey was filled with a deep anger and hatred toward the poachers who killed gorillas and interfered with her work.

Fossey did not get the greeting she had expected when she landed with all her baggage in Kigali. She found a frantic Alyette de Munck, alone. Halfway to Rwanda, de Munck and the three boys who were riding in an open jeep had met some friends, who had offered her a ride the rest of the way in their more comfortable car. She had accepted the ride. The boys, expected a day later, had never arrived. They had apparently taken a wrong turn, crossed into Congo, and been tortured and killed by Congolese soldiers. The tragedy infuriated Fossey, who was staying with Rosamond Carr at the time. Carr remembered Fossey's hysterical reaction when she learned of the boys' deaths:

> "We've got to find who did it!" she screamed. "I'm going to offer your houseboys money to go into the Congo to find out who did it!"
>
> I looked at her aghast. "Oh no you're not," I said. "No employee of mine is going into the Congo right now. It's far too dangerous. And besides," I added, "they won't go."
>
> "Oh yes, they will," she insisted. "Africans will do anything for money. You just watch. For a thousand francs, they'll do it."
>
> Dian pulled a thousand franc note from her purse and began to wave it around madly. "Who will go into the Congo for this money?" she shrieked. "Who will go and find out who murdered the son of Mrs. de Munck?"

Fossey's fury intensified; she threw more and more money into the air, still yelling, Carr translating, the onlookers dumbfounded. (Carr, 157–158)

Not one offered to go, and the incident only caused a rift between the two women. Fossey later wrote letters to friends urging others to avenge the murders, and swore she would do it herself if nobody else would; but the murderers were never identified. Her commitment to finding out who had killed the young men formed a bond between her and Alyette de Munck, who became the closest and most helpful friend in Fossey's life.

Together the two women buried their grief in the challenge ahead of them. They climbed Mount Visoke, in the shadow of Karisimbi, searching for a campsite. The climb was rigorous. Fossey's continued heavy smoking took a toll on her lungs, making them incapable of supplying the necessary oxygen to her muscles, which ached in protest. And, although she wouldn't admit it, Fossey suffered from acrophobia. If they came close to the edge of a cliff, or had to jump across a narrow ravine, she would freeze, unable to move without help.

De Munck, petite at 5'3" with short brown hair, and Fossey, towering above her with her 6' frame and long, black hair, made an odd-looking pair. After a two-hour climb they came to a small level meadow with a stony stream running through it. Tall moss-covered hagenia trees and dense bamboo surrounded the plateau where lobelias and wild orchids grew everywhere. Fossey called the small grass floor Karisoke, a name she created by combining the words Karisimbi and Visoke.

The women set up three tents, one that Fossey would live and work in, one for storage, and a small pup tent for occasional visitors. "I must say, despite the leaks, my canvas tent is a happy roof," wrote Fossey. (Matthews, 23) She and de Munck hired porters to bring up Fossey's supplies and equipment. Fossey had the same cook she had brought with her out of Congo and would hire two trackers and other workers from nearby villages.

Alyette de Munck came up the mountain often to visit and bring supplies. Fossey and de Munck supported each other at a time in their lives when they both needed someone. Together they explored the steep mountain slopes looking for gorillas, and shared the excitement when they found more than they could count.

Rosamond Carr also stayed overnight in the guest-tent from time to time. She remembered going out in the field for long days with Fossey to observe the mountain gorillas. The

Rosamond Halsey Carr, shown here in 1997, became one of Fossey's closest friends in Africa. Still, her first impression of Fossey may or may not have been a favorable one; she said that Fossey "conveyed in her demeanor no sense of friendliness or charm whatsoever, but rather a steely determination."

two dined on Oreo cookies and thermoses of hot tea to help ward off the rain forest's bone-chilling cold and dampness. Both Carr and de Munck provided warm, safe refuges in their homes when Fossey periodically came down the mountain for supplies or a respite.

In 1968 de Munck financed the first structure erected at Karisoke, a two-room cabin about 12' in width and 20' in length, covered with corrugated metal sheeting that was painted a dull green to blend with the nearby vegetation. It seemed like a castle after the tent in which Fossey had lived for two years. Fossey's new home had a fireplace, furniture, and doors and windows that she covered with curtains of bright yellow African printed cotton. Near the front door hung a machete that Fossey used to clear jungle paths. The new cabin was all that Fossey needed, and she was completely content.

She resumed her fieldwork, spending long hours each day identifying and counting Karisoke's gorilla population. By summer's end she had located nine gorilla groups and identified nearly 80 individual gorillas. At the end of each day she returned to the cabin, where her thoughts often turned to the Congolese soldiers. She had heard they were still looking for her. Fossey understood that if they captured her again she'd probably be killed. There were other problems at Karisoke. Just as she did at Kabara, Fossey had difficulties with the staff. Her cook grew surly. When she fired one of her workers, and he threatened her, she fired a warning shot over his head.

"WHO ASKED HIM TO RESCUE ME?"

Fossey had been at her camp only a few months when she was surprised by a visit from Alexie Forrester, her friend from Rhodesia. Fossey had written to him following the murders of de Munck's son and nephew and their friend. Fearing for her safety and health, Forrester tried to talk her into leaving with him. He wanted, he said, to marry her. But marriage was the furthest thing from Dian Fossey's mind. She had found her life's work, her reason for being. Karisoke was where she planned to stay. As much as she liked him, Fossey could not wait for Alexie to leave. He was interfering with her work, and that came first. As far as she was concerned, there was nothing outside of her gorillas that interested her, and she was not about to leave them.

Forrester knew more about Africa than Fossey. He was younger than she was, but he had grown up there and worked on the family farm, and he knew the Africa she did not know. Alarmed by Fossey's letter discussing revenge against the young Belgian men's murderers, Alexie left his studies at the University of Notre Dame to come to her, not to carry out her wish for revenge, but to persuade her to leave with him.

When that failed, Alexie tried to frighten her into leaving. She was a white woman, virtually alone in a remote camp in the mountains just miles from the Congo border, surrounded by native workers with thoughts and emotions she could not comprehend. Every time she chased some poachers, threatening them with her revolver, or tried to shoo away families intruding with their cattle on what she considered her territory, she was making new enemies.

Forrester told her he would not be surprised if she was herself murdered if she stayed. Fossey shook off the prediction. Unable to frighten her into leaving, he offered her advice. He told her she needed to scare the natives who believed in magical powers known as *sumu*, the Swahili word for malicious magic. Forrester suggested that she could persuade the natives that she was a witch so they'd be wary of her. "Get some Halloween masks, noisemakers, smoke bombs," he advised, "and use them."

"He came up here like Sir Galahad," Fossey wrote in her journal, "but who asked him to rescue me? He criticized everything here; said that the Rwandans hated me, that they called me a wild woman and wanted me out. Said I was making life impossible. . . . He as good as forced me to throw him out." (Mowat, 62)

RUNNING KARISOKE IN AN UNSTABLE LAND

Dian Fossey is thought of as a crusader against poaching, but it is important to remember that her environmental concerns were closely linked to politics —many suspect that her murder was itself political—and that Karisoke has not always managed to stay out of the region's political struggles. In 1997 and 1998, six Karisoke Research Center staff members lost their lives in the Rwandan civil war. Other staff members, such as Jean Bosco Bizumuremyi ("Bosco"), showed extreme bravery as the civil strife in Rwanda continued to affect Karisoke's workers.

Bosco, the son of Sebujangwe, Fossey's porter from 1968 until 1994, was hired to run Karisoke's camp in 1988. By 1993 he joined the center's anti-poaching team. The civil war had erupted in 1990 and by 1994 the fighting had escalated, forcing Karisoke's staff members to evacuate to Zaire. A United Nations convoy was sent to escort the staff members on their return to Rwanda, but when their arrival was delayed, the Karisoke staff, including Bosco, went to search for them. They were attacked by a group of Interahamwe militia, Rwandan rebels, armed with bayonets and machetes, and Bosco was injured severely enough to require a month's hospitalization.

In 1997, the Interahamwe militia looted Bosco's home and burned it to the ground. Throughout these ordeals, Bosco remained loyal to the research center and its mission of protecting the gorillas. Bosco serves today as Karisoke's liaison with National Park authorities in Rwanda. Like Dian Fossey's, Bosco's leadership is a product of his courage, selflessness, and devotion to the mountain gorillas he loves.

In scientific circles, professionals had long recognized the need to leave an isolated environment from time to time in order to maintain a healthy perspective on their studies. The lack of such a balanced life could impair their judgement and often resulted in what was called "going bushy." After nearly two years of such an existence, Fossey needed a break. She also needed a dentist, for constant toothaches made it impossible for her to eat anything but the softest foods. Dr. Leaky agreed that she should return to America for a brief time.

Prior to Fossey's departure for America, the National Geographic Society sent Alan Root to photograph Fossey and the gorillas for an article in an upcoming issue of its magazine, *National Geographic.* But constant rains prevented Root from getting the needed shots. Root had to return to his own work, but recommended that the National Geographic Society hire another nature photographer, Robert Campbell, of Nairobi, to complete the assignment. Bob Campbell, 40, was a former officer in the British army. Not only would Campbell be able to photograph the wildlife in Fossey's absence, he could look after the camp until she returned.

On September 24, 1968, Fossey left to return home to the United States. But as Fossey biographer Farley Mowat concluded in *Woman in the Mists,* the two years that Fossey had spent in Africa "had forged a different woman with a new life, and there was now some doubt as to where 'home' really was." (70)

6

The Path to Celebrity: 1968–1970

COCO AND PUCKER PUSS

Fossey returned to Karisoke in December of 1968. While in America, she had visited the Henry family and her mother and stepfather, but she had left feeling annoyed by all of them. They seemed to her to be preoccupied with their own interests, which Fossey considered small and unimportant. "Gorillas are almost altruistic in nature," she told an interviewer. "There's very little, if any, 'me-itis.' When I get back to civilization, I'm always appalled by 'me, me, me.'" ("Zoologist Is Slain," 15)

No one seemed to comprehend the importance of her study of the mountain gorillas. Although her parents were proud of her growing fame, they were deeply worried about her safety.

While Fossey was impatient with individuals not well versed in primatology, she was eager to discuss her gorilla studies with those who truly shared the excitement of her pioneering work. She met with officials at the National Geographic Society in

Fossey photographs the orphaned Coco and Pucker Puss, "the babies," who lived in Fossey's cabin at Karisoke while recovering from encounters with poachers. She formed a strong bond with them and learned from them a great deal about gorilla behavior. She was devastated to lose them to the Cologne Zoo: "There is no way," she wrote, "to describe the pain of their loss."

Washington, who were greatly impressed by her groundbreaking data. Before returning to Africa, she also met with Robert Hinde in England. Hinde, the head of graduate studies in animal behavior at Cambridge University, had guided Jane Goodall in her chimpanzee study. Dr. Leakey had urged Fossey, now 36, to begin a doctoral program under Hinde's direction and had arranged for him to visit Karisoke. While she was not enthusiastic, Fossey realized that the advanced degree was essential to enhance the credibility of her work.

Back at Karisoke, Fossey said goodbye to Bob Campbell, the *National Geographic* photographer who had overseen the camp in Fossey's absence. Although Campbell would frequently return to Karisoke to photograph in the next several years, he and his wife made their home in Nairobi.

Fossey, now 37, was delighted to be alone in the camp once more. She threw herself into her work again, and set out to locate the gorilla groups that she had earlier identified. In addition to identifying gorilla families, she had given many individual group members names, usually assigning a moniker that fit a gorilla for some behavioral or physical characteristics: Brahms, Bartok, Beethoven, Icarus, Digit, Whinny, Peanuts, Samson, Geezer, Rafiki (Swahili for *friend*), and Uncle Bert, an older, nurturing silverback whom she named for her favorite uncle in California.

On February 24, 1969, Fossey returned to camp with her tracker to find an urgent message from a doctor in Ruhengeri, a nearby town. The message informed Fossey that a young gorilla had been captured and was being held at the park conservator's office. The next morning Fossey made the trip to Ruhengeri, where she found a 16-month-old female crouching in a cage. The young gorilla was very ill, and Fossey persuaded the conservator to allow her to take the sick, terrified animal to Karisoke, where she'd care for her. Although Fossey was outraged by the circumstances surrounding the infant's abduction, there was little time to protest. The baby was badly dehydrated and needed immediate care.

Fossey called the gorilla Coco, after an older female who had recently died, and kept her inside her cabin. She had her workers create a jungle-like environment in the room next to Fossey's bedroom by covering the floor with nesting vegetation. Vines were strung from the ceiling so that the youngster could swing to and fro. "Eventually [she] sits down to peer longingly through the window that faces the slopes of Mount Visoke just a few hundred yards away," she wrote, "and there [she] finally cries [herself] to sleep in pathetic body-wracking sobs. Coco, my first infant gorilla charge, is at home." ("Making Friends," 56)

Fossey feared that her young charge wouldn't survive. After Coco's first night at Karisoke, Fossey awoke to find her asleep. She left her for about an hour and later described what she saw upon her return: "Opening the door, I found instead complete chaos. The 'gorilla proof' matting the men had nailed over the camp's stock of food supplies, stored in shelves along one wall of Coco's room, had been torn away from the storage cupboards. In the midst of an array of tin cans and opened boxes Coco sat contentedly sampling sugar, flour, jam, rice, and spaghetti. My momentary dismay at the havoc she had created was instantly replaced with delight upon realizing that she somehow had had the curiosity and energy to create such a mess." (*Gorillas in the Mist*, 111)

A week later, poachers arrived at Karisoke carrying a large barrel. Inside was another young, sick gorilla, an emaciated two-year-old female that Fossey named Pucker Puss, or Pucker. Pucker's head bore machete wounds, and on her wrists and ankles were deep cuts caused by wire bindings. Fossey later learned that many adult gorillas had been killed by the poachers while fighting to defend the infants.

Coco and Pucker, whom Fossey referred to as "the babies," shared the jungle room in Fossey's cabin. Both required constant care. She concocted a medicated formula of "gorilla milk" and fed them with baby bottles. The camp's cook quit in disgust, telling Fossey in Swahili, "I am a cook for Europeans, not animals." (*Gorillas in the Mist*, 114)

During Coco and Pucker's recovery, Fossey learned much about gorilla behavior. She developed an intimate relationship with her two young charges that transcended anything Fossey had previously experienced in her fieldwork. She watched their gestures and listened to their vocalizations, which provided her with new and valuable insights that resulted in a breakthrough in Fossey's knowledge and understanding of mountain gorillas.

When Fossey initially agreed to care for Coco and Pucker, she promised to return them to the conservator when they recovered, hoping that eventually she'd be able to persuade him to allow her to keep the pair. She planned to return them to the wild where a gorilla group would adopt them. Later, Fossey learned that the young gorillas were to be sent to the Cologne

Coco and Pucker were orphans; their parents had died, presumably, in trying to defend them from poachers. Mountain gorillas can be fierce in defending their young from strangers, but they relax when their group has no young to protect. It was with such a relaxed group that Fossey practiced the vocalizations she'd learned from the orphans.

Zoo in Germany. As Fossey nursed Coco and Pucker back to health, she wrote frantic letters to Cologne's mayor asking that the zoo cancel the animals' purchase. But her pleas were ignored. Finally, the conservator *ordered* Fossey to return Coco and Pucker. Their loss was a bitter blow. After they were taken from Karisoke, she wrote, "I ran out of the cabin . . . [and] deep into the forest until I could run no more. There is no way to describe the pain of their loss." (Matthews, 35)

Coco and Pucker were flown to the Cologne Zoo, where they were caged together; they died in 1978, within one month of each other. No mountain gorillas yet have lived long lives or produced young in captivity.

THE FAMOUS HANDSHAKE

Two days after Pucker and Coco left Karisoke, Fossey returned to the field. She was concerned that during her two-month absence while caring for the two infants, the gorilla groups might have forgotten her. She first approached Group 8, a somewhat unusual family led by Rafiki, an elderly silverback. Group 8's clan had no babies, so the adults were less defensive and more comfortable with Fossey's presence among them. She tried a deep, throaty vocalization—"*Naoom, naoom, naoom*"—that she had seen Coco and Pucker use while eating. Fossey noted that the sage silverback greeted her with a look of mild amusement. "Rafiki came up to me with an expression that seemed to say, 'Come on, now. You can't fool me.' They had not forgotten me." ("Making Friends," 58) Thanks to Pucker and Coco, Fossey's newly refined mimicry and vocalization skills provided even greater acceptance among the gorillas. Eventually, she discovered that gorillas communicated with at least 25 vocalizations. While in the field, Fossey carefully recorded these on a portable tape recorder.

Fossey added the "belch vocalization" to her growing repertoire of sounds, a burp that usually signified contentment. She also came to understand that gorillas used belches for a variety of purposes. For instance, a brief belch was used to discipline the young, just as adult humans often clear their throats to attract a child's attention when a youngster is too noisy in a quiet place. When gorillas belched back and forth to one another within the group, these sounds signaled their physical location within the group.

In addition to belches, there were grunts. Fossey observed that juveniles used a "pig grunt," to say "you're playing too rough," while females used it to settle small disputes or to discipline their young. The silverbacks emitted the pig grunt to referee disputes among other adult gorillas. Fossey also identified the "hoot bark," a silverback's method of getting everyone's attention either to make his presence known or to signal alarm.

While Fossey's tape recordings and her hundreds of pages of notes covering over 2,000 hours of observations were vital field study records, they had to be backed by photographic documentation. It was during this critical phase of Fossey's work that Robert Campbell returned to Karisoke from time to time to photograph Fossey with the mountain gorillas for *National Geographic.* She resented the intrusion of anyone staying in her camp other than her friends Carr and de Munck, but she realized that Campbell's photographs were imperative to the recording of her work.

Still, Fossey often sank into her characteristic surliness. She was rude to the photographer and did everything she could to make his visits to Karisoke as miserable as possible. She would lead the way into the field as, puffing and sweating under their warm clothes, every muscle aching, the two climbed a thousand feet up the mountain. They would then sit for hours in the cold drizzle, watching, even when there was no indication that gorillas might be nearby. During these long hours spent waiting, Campbell was forced to sit as motionless as Fossey, who seemed to be trying to antagonize him. She was ill-tempered, rebuffing his efforts to be friendly, which drove him to dine alone in his tent and avoid Fossey except when they were working. At one point, Campbell was ready to quit and go home to Nairobi.

It took about three months for Fossey and Robert Campbell to become accustomed to working together while preserving their independence. The more he watched Fossey work, the more he admired her strength and dedication. She in turn gradually began to welcome his company, and she appreciated his expertise in his field and enthusiasm for filming. She spent long nights at her typewriter, writing the articles for *National Geographic* that would be illustrated by his photographs.

It was during this time that Campbell photographed the most extraordinary moment in Fossey's career. Just after Christmas of that year, Alyette de Munck had climbed to Karisoke for the day, and Campbell and the two women went to the area where they had often seen Group 8 gathered. Campbell and de Munck stayed behind a Hagenia tree while Fossey slowly crawled toward the gorillas, then lay motionless.

One of the gorillas was Peanuts, a curious, playful young blackback. "Peanuts left his tree for a bit of strutting before he began his approach," Fossey wrote. "He is a showman. He beat his chest; he threw leaves in the air; he swaggered and slapped the foliage around him; and then suddenly was at my side. His

NAMING THE GORILLAS

When Dian Fossey began her work with mountain gorillas, the scientific custom was to identify animals by numbers, such as infant 2 in Group 6. But Fossey followed the controversial new method that Jane Goodall had initiated in her studies of the chimpanzees of Gombe. Goodall, looking to develop a more humanistic approach to primate research, assigned human or human-like names to her chimps, such as Fifi and Passion. Fossey copied this technique, naming gorillas according to their physical features (Digit) or personality traits (Puck).

This practice continues today at the Karisoke Research Center, where staff members assign gorilla infants names that carry special meaning in their native language. For instance, an infant born in April of 2000 was named Afrika, for the Karisoke staff's sadness over prolonged civil conflicts in the Democratic Republic of the Congo. Similarly, an infant born in 1999 was named Imvune ("infiltrations"), referring to the difficult conditions the research center's trackers encountered during the region's ongoing fighting. When, in 2000, a 19-year-old female finally gave birth to her first surviving infant, the baby was named Pato ("to wait"). Later that year, another infant was named in honor of Dian Fossey and her commitment to conservation.

expression indicated that he had entertained me—now it was my turn." ("More Years," 575–576)

Peanuts eyed Fossey as she chewed some leaves. When he scratched, she scratched. "It was not clear who was aping whom," she wrote. ("More Years," 576) Then Fossey slowly stretched her arm out on the ground.

They all waited motionless, to see what would happen. Peanuts gazed at the hand, took a step toward it, then reached out and briefly touched the hand. "Peanuts seemed to ponder accepting my hand," Fossey later wrote in *National Geographic.* " . . . [He] gently touched his fingers to mine. . . . To the best of my knowledge this is the first time a wild gorilla had ever come so close to 'holding hands' with a human being." Peanuts' handshake with Fossey was a result of three years of intensive fieldwork— and Campbell had captured it on film. ("More Years," 576)

As 1970 began, Fossey reluctantly left for England to begin her studies at Cambridge University, where she spent the next three months. She disliked England's chilly, damp climate— although in many ways it was much like that of the rain forest—and she disliked the crowds and the traffic. Unable to find quarters in a remote setting, Fossey was forced to live in a noisy dormitory filled with students. She studied statistical analysis, a subject she found utterly boring. But Fossey's bleak winter in Cambridge was brightened when her first article for *National Geographic,* "Making Friends with Mountain Gorillas," appeared in the January 1970 issue and made the cover of the famous publication. Although Fossey's work was already known in the scientific community, it was the *National Geographic* exposure that brought public attention to Fossey and the plight of the mountain gorilla.

THE EFFECTS OF CELEBRITY
Fossey soon realized that she had become a public figure. That summer she made another trip, this time to the United States, where she found that she had attained celebrity status in

This is one of Bob Campbell's most famous photographs, of the very moment of "the famous handshake" between Fossey and Peanuts. Fossey was inviting Peanuts to be comfortable around her—even chewing leaves—when she decided to try for physical contact. After three years' work, the attempt was a major success.

academic and anthropology circles. Her public appearances began to draw people who were much like she had been in the early 1960s: young men and women seeking a challenging experience, yearning to come to Africa to work for her and

The Gorilla Girl in Washington, D.C. in September of 1970, with a photograph of one of her research subjects. As Fossey's reputation grew, she was forced to deal with ever greater interference from the outside world, interference that she would have been happier without. Still, the increased support enabled her to turn Karisoke into a powerful advocate for the preservation of the gorillas she had come to think of as friends.

to study at Karisoke. It had been just four years since she had gone to listen to Louis Leakey lecture in Louisville. Guests at a fundraising banquet in that city paid $1,000 each to hear Fossey speak.

Over the next 15 years, dozens of American and British students would come to Karisoke, some to conduct the gorilla census, identifying and counting each gorilla, while others came to photograph and study. Some would return several times, thriving on the challenge and adventure and producing impressive studies that would launch their own successful careers as primatologists. Others would quickly realize that life in the rough was not for them, or they were sent packing by an impatient Dian Fossey. Many students found her aloof, too demanding, and too difficult to get along with. "She discouraged distractions of any kind," said Rosamond Carr, who recalled Fossey's troubled relationships with students and interns, "such as excursions down the mountain or close relationships among the students." (Carr, 171)

Although Fossey often questioned the dedication of the visiting students, she also recognized the potential value of their assistance to the gorilla project. With their help, Fossey realized her ambition to turn Karisoke into a top-rated research center. Fossey's entire vision for the research center and her role there was expanding. With thoughts of Coco and Pucker and countless other victims of the relentless gorilla poaching always with her, Fossey's goals began to change from studying the mountain gorillas to protecting and observing them. Fossey concluded her second article for *National Geographic* with a discussion of the importance of a gorilla census:

> One reason for the census is to underscore the need for protection of these rare creatures. As if to underscore it further, when I returned to camp I was greeted with news of a wholesale gorilla slaughter just south of my study area. The bodies of five animals were found scattered about in an arc of some 75 yards. They had been mauled by dogs, pierced by spears, and battered by stones, apparently just for the excitement of the hunt. I think of the gorillas I have written about, whom I have come to regard as friends, and I wonder—will some of them be next?

> ("More Years," 585)

7

Saving the Gorillas: 1970–1978

CAMPBELL, CAMBRIDGE, AND ACTIVISM

When photographer Bob Campbell had first arrived at Karisoke in 1969, Fossey had treated him with contempt. In the following months, her attitude had gradually changed. Her hostility had melted into friendship, and by 1970 she was in love with him.

Fossey's published articles and books reveal little about her love affair with Campbell, who was married. But her journal entries and the accounts of friends reveal the depth of Fossey's love for him. Rosamond Carr called Fossey's time with Campbell "the happiest years of Fossey's life." (Carr, 161)

Campbell and Fossey continued to spend endless hours in the field. Their collaborative efforts were documented in Fossey's second article, "More Years With Mountain Gorillas," in the October 1971 issue of *National Geographic*. The article included Campbell's unique and marvelous pictures of the

Fossey with gorilla skulls seized from poachers in the forest. As the years of her research passed, Fossey's study of the gorillas became first friendship with them and then a ferocious drive to protect them from poachers. In her activism she parted ways with some friends and members of the scientific community—and made enemies among the Africans.

moment when the young male gorilla, Peanuts, reached out to touch Fossey's hand.

Her happiness while working in the field with Campbell is reflected in her description of their excursions. "The physical challenges involved covering each of the six Virunga mountains from saddle to summit exploring every gully, ravine, and slope. . . . Personally, I found the explorations throughout the volcanoes some if my most memorable forest experiences—the challenge of the search, the thrill of encountering a new gorilla group, the awesome beauty of the mountains revealed by virtually every turn in a trail, and the pleasure of making a 'home' with only a tent and the benevolence of nature." (*Gorillas in the Mist*, 157, 158)

Campbell spent almost three years at the research center. Fossey hoped that he would leave his wife, marry her, and remain at Karisoke—but it was not to be. Early in 1972, Fossey returned to America to visit her parents. While she was away, Campbell left the camp and went home to Nairobi. He never returned to Karisoke. Campbell later called the gorilla project the highlight of his professional career.

Fossey was devastated by Campbell's departure. "Never have I known such sorrow," she wrote in her journal. The loss marked a critical turning point in Fossey's life and work. In many ways, she was never the same again. She stopped studying the gorillas with the same intensity she had brought to her work before then.

During the next two years, Fossey completed her doctoral studies at Cambridge University, earning a doctoral degree in zoology in 1974. But the degree meant little to her now. She had forced herself to plug the carefully documented data on almost every aspect of gorilla behavior into the required statistical format, and she had hated the work. From that time on, Fossey completed only four articles for scientific journals.

Fossey's doctoral thesis remains an important contribution in the field of primatology. "Her dissertation on mountain gorillas really established the baseline for grammatologists' understanding of the species," observed George Schaller, the eminent zoologist who had marked the first study of the great apes. "[Fossey] contributed a vast amount of information about what was largely an unknown ape," writes Phyllis Jay Dolhinow, a biological anthropologist at the University of California at Berkeley. "Her paradigms were not fashionable, not quantitative, but that's okay. She was an accurate reporter and reported it well." (Morell et al., 422)

After completing her work at Cambridge, Fossey returned to Karisoke. She began to spend the bulk of her time directing the work of the many graduate students who came to study with her. But Fossey's dark moods became more frequent, and her relationships with the students deteriorated. The most visible sign of Fossey's increasing bitterness was a shift in the focus of her work. She showed little interest in the daily reports of the gorilla groups. Instead, she poured all her attention and energy into fighting poachers. Kelly Stewart, a student who was there at the time, reported, "If anyone did anything other than going out on anti-poaching patrols, she labeled them as selfish. And compared to her, other people were more interested in their own research and less in the conservation. But that was her whole life."

Foiling hunters' traps became Fossey's passion. Native hunters set snares to trap animals for meat, not gorillas. They were after a small red antelope called a duiker, and the water buffalo. But the traps set by the local Batwa tribesmen occasionally caught a gorilla. Other tribes, especially the Bahutu, cut down trees to get at bees' nests for honey, destroying one source of the gorillas' food. The hunters' activities scared the gorillas into fleeing, interrupting the work of Fossey and her students.

In addition to the hunters, herdsmen drove their cattle wherever they pleased, sometimes right through the middle of her camp. They invaded the gorillas' parkland sanctuary, sending them scurrying for safety. All of this infuriated Fossey, but she reserved her fiercest hatred for the poachers who targeted the gorillas themselves. She urged the Rwandan government to hire more park guards and authorize them to shoot poachers on sight. She advocated killing some of the cows any time a herd wandered into park grounds. If they came back, she said, kill more of them. If the officials wouldn't do it, she would.

To her critics in Rwanda, this foreign white woman was placing the value of useless gorillas over the survival of the native tribes whose numbers and need for food were growing. They were right. Nothing meant more to her than the survival of the remaining 270 mountain gorillas in the only place on earth where they could be found.

THE FIGHT AGAINST POACHERS

Fossey's campaign against the poachers had started in the spring of 1970, just after her return from Cambridge. Bob Campbell had scared away some herdsmen and their cattle by firing a pistol over their heads; one bullet even grazed a herdsman. While Fossey was in the United States in the summer of 1970, she left a British graduate student, Alan Goodall, in charge of Karisoke. Goodall discovered a small group of poachers and, caught up in the anti-poacher spirit, first fired warning shots over their heads and then wounded two of them.

A few months later, Fossey herself chased some Watusies who had cut the hind legs of a water buffalo and left it to struggle. She fired at them from too great a distance to hit them. One of the men was a worker at Karisoke; understandably, he never came back.

But the incident led to the killing of six of Fossey's gorillas, whose bodies were found in a village at the foot of the mountain. Fossey asked Alyette de Munck to find out how it had happened. De Munck investigated and reported that Bahutu and Batwa tribesmen had chased the gorillas down the mountain and killed them with bows and arrows. Their motive was revenge for the shooting of the two poachers.

Fossey preferred to believe that the gorillas had been killed while defending a baby from being kidnapped. Taking the gorillas back to Karisoke, she invited scientists from

THE REALITIES OF POACHING

Despite international concern, poachers continue to kill gorillas. On May 9, 2002, gunshots were heard in the Rwandan jungle, and on the following day, guards discovered the bodies of two female adults. One of these was 25-year-old Muraha, whose mother Dr. Fossey had studied and whom Dr. Fossey had named herself, after a volcano that erupted at the time of Muraha's birth. Muraha's 13-month-old infant, Ubuzima, was clinging to her body.

The body of another female, 11-year-old Impanga, was nearby. Her first infant, Bibisi, was missing, probably abducted. Impanga had twice survived death by antelope snare, but she had lost a hand and a foot in the process. Although handicapped, Impanga became an excellent mother to Bibisi. (Bibisi was named for the British Broadcasting Corporation, or BBC, which was filming at the time of her birth.)

Before this incident, such poaching had not been experienced in Rwanda for nearly two decades. The Convention on International Trade in Endangered Species (CITES) has now banned all commercial trade in gorillas, and no reputable zoo would accept a wild-caught ape—but the International Primate Protection League (IPPL) recently obtained a Nigerian dealer's list offering $1.6 million for an infant gorilla's head. "What gorilla mother is safe," asks the IPPL's chairperson, Dr. Shirley McGreal, "with a bounty of nearly half a million dollars on her baby's head?"

Cambridge to come and study the specimens.

News of the shootings and the gorilla slayings sent tremors through the halls and offices of the National Geographic Society in Washington, undermining her support. At one point, the Society decided to cut off her funding, which left her with no money to pay her workers or buy food. Her grant was renewed only after Robert Campbell intervened for her.

Fossey's temper was infamous. She would not hesitate to yell at trackers or other staff if she suspected them of stealing from her or not doing their work to her satisfaction. She could act like a crazy woman, so it seemed to them, and that was totally intentional.

Fossey had never forgotten Alexie Forrester's advice to her about frightening the natives with black magic. He had suggested that she get some masks to frighten them. While on a trip to the United States, Fossey had purchased some Halloween masks.

When Fossey returned to Africa, she visited Rosamond Carr and showed the masks to her friend. One especially grotesque mask was that of a witch. It featured long, ugly teeth and eyes that bulged out of their sockets. The bulging eyes were attached to a rubber ball that Fossey could squeeze, causing the eyes to protrude. When Fossey wore it in front of Carr's native house staff, they were frightened. Sembagare, Carr's trusted house servant, told Carr, "Madame, if she wears that mask in the mountain, they will surely kill her. The first man who sees her will throw a spear right through her heart." (Carr, 174)

Soon afterward, Fossey wore the mask to scare some poachers she and her staff had rounded up and brought into camp. If they believed she was a witch and thought she had some kind of supernatural powers, then so much the better; that was the way she wanted it. Once, it backfired on her. One of the local tribes brought a sick child to her and, believing she had such powers, asked her to cure it. She did not know what to do for the child and sent them away.

Fossey's relationship with the Rwandan authorities deteriorated as her anti-poaching crusade gained momentum. In 1976 *National Geographic* produced a film, *Gorilla*, that featured some footage of Fossey filmed by Bob Campbell. Hoping to improve the relationship between Fossey and the locals, U.S. Ambassador Crigler arranged for a showing of the film. He invited Fossey and the members of Rwanda's cabinet to attend.

Fossey arrived wearing a stunning outfit that featured a white silk blouse and a black lace skirt. She was charming to the assembled guests. Ambassador Crigler's hopes for improving Fossey's reputation among the officials seemed to have been realized until the question-and-answer session that followed the film. As more and more questions were directed at Fossey about her stance against the poachers, her temper flared. "They should be hung," Fossey said about the poachers. "She then lunged forward and made a neck-breaking gesture with her hands around her neck," recalled Rosamond Carr, "and shouted, '*Hung!*'" (175)

Rosamond Carr and Alyette de Munck had lived in Africa for many years and understood much more about its culture than Fossey. For several years they had tried to persuade their friend that the natives had a right to farm the land and trap wild game to feed their families. But Fossey refused to listen. "I had conflicting feelings about Fossey's anti-poaching activities," wrote Carr. "I was at the same time awed by her bravery, appalled by her tactics, and genuinely frightened for her safety and welfare. This was a country where such interference by a foreign visitor was looked upon with considerable resentment, and I felt there should have been more flexibility on her part." (Carr, 174)

Fossey in the "gorilla graveyard" in which she herself would ultimately be laid to rest. All the graves contain friends of hers among the gorilla populations, many of them slain by the poachers whose illegal activities she was struggling to stop.

THE DEATH OF DIGIT

During her years at Karisoke, Fossey had developed a special relationship with the gorilla family she identified as Group 4. She witnessed vast changes within the group, including births, deaths, and the movement of three younger females into the family. More than any other group studied by Fossey, they provided her with a long-term record of changes within a single group.

Group 4 was led by Uncle Bert, a silverback who'd become the family's leader following the death of their former patriarch, Whinny. At first, Fossey believed Uncle Bert would be a cold, undemonstrative father, but she was wrong. The silverback proved to be an effective leader and a caring parent. Fossey wrote in *National Geographic* that "the character of a group is frequently determined by the character of its leader." ("Making Friends," 60)

Fossey was fond of the group's youngsters, who readily accepted her. Her favorite was a young male she called Digit because of his crooked, broken, finger. Digit and Fossey shared a special bond. She first came to know the friendly gorilla when he was a baby. Over time, she watched him mature into a huge blackback who assumed a role of responsibility within his group. Time and change did not diminish the bond between Fossey and Digit. In fact, their friendship deepened.

Fossey spent many hours with Group 4, playing with the youngsters, grooming members of the family, and allowing herself to be groomed. Her increased involvement with the gorillas draws some criticism from the magazine *Science*: "[A]s Fossey went from dispassionate observer to participant in gorilla social life [tickling infants, letting the gorillas rummage in her belongings and groom her], she grew less interested in science. The final straw for her was the fact that the gorillas (then numbering only 250) were in danger of being wiped out by poachers and civilization itself." (Morell et al., 424)

On January 1, 1978, Fossey's longtime tracker Nemeye returned from the field to report that he was unable to locate Group 4. The next day, Fossey, a visiting student named Ian Redmond, and two trackers set out to search for the family. It was Redmond who discovered Digit's mutilated body. His head, hands, and feet had been hacked off, and multiple spear wounds pierced his body. Redmond had the difficult task of breaking the news to Fossey, who recounts her own reaction best in *Gorillas in the Mist* (206):

> There are times when one cannot accept facts for fear of shattering one's being. . . . [A]ll of Digit's life, since my first meeting with him as a playful little ball of black fluff ten years earlier, passed through my mind. From that moment on, I came to live within an insulated part of myself.
>
>   . . . Digit took five mortal spear wounds into his body, held off six poachers and their dogs in order to allow his family members, including his mate Simba and their unborn infant, to flee. . . . Digit's last battle had been a lonely and courageous one. During his valiant struggle he managed to kill one of the poachers' dogs before dying. I have tried not to allow myself to think of Digit's anguish, pain, and the total comprehension he must have suffered in knowing what humans were doing to him.

GOODALL ON FOSSEY

She was really something—putting on masks, chasing people, kidnapping them. If only she had embraced humanity a little more . . . she could still be here. She was quite different when she was in America, very sweet. But she didn't like people going near her and the gorillas. I had these long talks with her and begged her, "Dian, why don't you involve the poachers in your research? Let them see the gorillas, help them understand." She said, "No, no, then the gorillas will be even more vulnerable."

—Primatologist Jane Goodall

Fossey and her coworkers at Karisoke, behind a table laden with snares they have removed from the area's forests. Even since her death, Fossey's work to save the endangered mountain gorillas has brought about a promising increase in their populations. According to Birute Galdikas, Louis Leakey's choice to carry out his study of orangutans, "[W]ithout her work, it is doubtful that mountain gorillas would have survived" into the 21st century.

The gorilla's body was returned to Fossey's camp, where it was buried not far from her own cabin. "To bury his body," Fossey affirmed, "was not to bury his memory."

8

No One Loved Gorillas More: 1978–1985

Perhaps in death Dian Fossey will achieve what eluded her in life: absolute protection for the mountain gorillas. In her devotion to these animals, Dian will be remembered for generations as one of the heroes of the twentieth century. Without her work, it is doubtful that mountain gorillas would have survived to the twenty-first.
—**Primatologist Birute Galdikas**

NOT TO HAVE DIED IN VAIN

Thousands of miles from Rwanda, millions of Americans watched the CBS evening news on February 3, 1978, just as they did most evenings. But that night's lead story was not about the White House or Congress. Walter Cronkite opened the program with the news of Digit's death. Many of those viewers had recently seen the new *National Geographic* film special about mountain gorillas that featured Dian Fossey and Digit.

Fossey's work with the gorillas of the Virungas, especially with their vocalizations, changed the face of primate research, and in the process she developed strong emotional bonds with many of her subjects, leading to her costly mission to save them from poachers. Some have criticized Fossey's work as less than absolutely scientific—but the effect of her struggle has been to save the species.

Not only was the news of Digit's tragic death a powerful story, it was an incredible event in the history of wildlife conservation. Just a few years earlier, no one knew or cared about the mountain gorillas' existence. Because of Dian

Fossey, they now knew of the gorillas' plight. They even knew a gorilla by name.

Following Digit's burial in the cemetery at Karisoke, Fossey and Ian Redmond discussed ways to combat the increasing menace of the poachers. Redmond advocated publicizing Digit's death to draw attention to the need for cooperation between Rwanda and Zaire—Congo had been renamed Zaire in October of 1971, as part of a social and political movement to expel colonial European influence—so that the same laws would be enforced throughout the Virungas. Fossey hesitated. She realized that the publicity might raise a lot of money. But how would it be used? She had lived in the mountains for 11 years and understood that the local officials did not see wildlife conservation as a pressing need. Her greatest fear was that any funds generated for this cause would be squandered; that would be an insult to the dignity of Digit's life and to his death.

Lying awake that night, Fossey grappled with the question of publicity. "The black night skies faded into those of a gray-misted dawn," she later recalled, "when I realized that, like Ian, I did not want Digit to have died in vain. I decided to launch a Digit Fund to support active conservation of gorillas, the money only to be used to expand antipoacher foot patrols within the park. This would involve the recruitment, training, outfitting, and remuneration of Africans willing to work long tedious hours cutting down traplines and confiscating poacher weapons such as spears, bows, and arrows."

Fossey wrote dozens of letters to heads of governments and the media throughout the world. They responded. As she had predicted, contributions poured in to the Digit Fund.

The donors saw Fossey as a gentle, loving woman who had gone to Africa and devoted her life to the preservation of mountain gorillas. They did not know that Fossey had declared a full-scale war on the poachers who had killed Digit. The identification and punishment of poachers had become her reason for living.

REVENGE

Within a week after Digit's death, Fossey's workers located a suspect, a man who carried a bloodstained bow and some arrows. Alone with the captive, Fossey later admitted, she tortured him until he confessed to Digit's murder and gave her the other poachers' names. Then she turned him over to the park guards.

Fossey became obsessed with revenge. Every suspected poacher brought to her was "interviewed," the word she wrote in her diary using quotation marks to mean tortured and whipped, until he confessed and named other poachers. The government fined her for these actions, but that didn't stop Fossey. Only the fear of being thrown out of the country restrained her at all.

The local tribes had their own thoughts of revenge. The crazy white woman who towered over them—they called her the *mzungu,* a Swahili term for a foreigner, a Caucasian person, or, in this case, a person different from the locals—had humiliated and tortured them long enough.

On July 24, 1978 one of Karisoke's four visiting students knocked on Fossey's door. When she saw the horrified look on his face, Fossey immediately knew that another gorilla atrocity had taken place. Uncle Bert had been murdered, shot through the heart and decapitated. Later, they discovered that a female named Macho had also been shot and killed. Her baby, Kweli, was wounded. "All the horror and shock of Digit's murder had returned," Fossey wrote in her diary, "and I felt I was going to go mad."

Fossey accused park officials of killing the gorillas; only the guards had rifles. Some of the students believed this slaughter was done in revenge against Dian Fossey. Others disagreed, but that's the way most people saw it. More important, that's the way the Rwandan government saw it.

The "wild woman of the Virungas," who had sworn to protect the few remaining gorillas from extinction, was now seen as causing more of them to die.

At about that time, when Fossey was away from the camp one night, someone cut a hole in the side of her cabin and stole most of her possessions. She reacted with more fury than ever, and this only increased concern over her mental and physical condition. She had become an embarrassment to the American government, the Leakey Foundation, and the National Geographic Society, and was considered a threat to the tranquility of Rwanda.

THE END OF THE WORLD

Dian Fossey had made the gorillas and Karisoke famous all over the world. This had an unexpected and unwanted result. Tourists began to flock to Kigali to see them. Self-styled guides charged hundreds of dollars to bring sightseers up the mountain, which made Fossey even angrier. Suddenly the government saw a bright new source of revenue: a camp—her camp—where tourists could stay overnight and view the famous gorillas by day. Only Dian Fossey, the person who had made it all possible, stood in the way.

It remained for one of her former students to come up with a plan that would satisfy everyone—with the exception, of course, of Dian Fossey, who wanted only to be left alone with her gorillas.

Alexander Harcourt had been one of Fossey's brightest student-assistants. He had spent parts of three years at Karisoke, and was now a celebrated primatologist. Harcourt reasoned that a lack of money and food was what drove the local tribes to kill gorillas and move into the parklands with their cattle. Find another source of income for them, and the gorillas would no longer be threatened. In fact, if the source of income was tourists coming just to see the gorillas, it would be to everyone's advantage to protect those gorillas.

The work at Karisoke has been impeded by political unrest in the region, but visitors now tour the Virungas consistently. The gorilla groups move around quite a bit, so visitors hire guides familiar with the area to lead them to likely sites. The trek to the site can take five or six hours, and the visit with the gorillas may be only a brief one.

Thus the Mountain Gorilla Project was born. The first step was for scientists to get Fossey's gorilla groups accustomed to the presence of more humans than they had seen with Fossey's staff. The next step would be to limit the number of tourists at each viewing, to avoid alarming the gorillas. The cabins at Karisoke would be renovated to provide rustic but adequate accommodations. Harcourt and his wife, who had met at Karisoke, would be in charge of the camp.

Fossey tried every argument she could think of to shoot down the project, but nobody was convinced. At 46, she was sick and unable to continue her work in the field. Fossey had neglected her health for years. Even before Bob Campbell's arrival at the camp in 1969, Fossey had refused treatment for broken bones. Instead, she hobbled around with a walking stick. Sometimes the broken bones healed improperly and later required surgery. Once, bitten by a rabid dog, she had refused to seek the necessary rabies shots until the resulting illness had become severe. Now, in the prime of her life, Fossey's feet were riddled with hairline fractures that made walking painful. The years of chain-smoking had battered her lungs, and advanced emphysema often prevented her from leaving her cabin. Although she had visited Group 4 for a time after Digit's murder, his death effectively marked the end of Fossey's active participation in field studies. Instead, she depended upon Karisoke's students to keep her informed.

While the world celebrated what she had accomplished, she saw only the end of *her* world. But where could she go? Her book was unfinished; what could she do? The answer came when Glenn Hauffater, a professor at Cornell University who visited Karisoke in August of 1979, offered her a position as a visiting professor and lecturer at Cornell. Fossey accepted the offer.

She left Karisoke for three months to arrange for her departure. When she returned to pack her belongings, she learned that her pet monkey, Kima, had died and her dog, Cindy, was sick. The following morning, porters carried her possessions down the mountain to a waiting truck. Some of her staff who had been with her for a decade or longer saw her off.

Nobody asked them what they were thinking as the *mzungu* disappeared from view.

In the small college town of Ithaca, New York, Dian Fossey was a fish out of water, alone in a strange land. She lived in a tiny student-housing apartment surrounded by exuberant students of less than half her age. At night she wrote, carefully answering every letter she received from scientists and schoolchildren alike. She was at her best when giving her lectures, which kept her listeners spellbound. She was at her worst in trying to organize and produce a book that was compelling and sufficiently scientific, yet captured the flavor of her life with the mountain gorillas of the Virungas. The project was a hopeless mess.

Her friend Anita McClellan, who owned the rights to it, saw that the book was unfit for publication. She persuaded Fossey to spend the summer of 1981 with her in a cabin in Maine, where they could finish the work with no distractions. McClellan managed gradually to pull from Fossey the painful and exhilarating stories that became the best-selling *Gorillas in the Mist*. When the project ended, Fossey longed to return to the mountain that she considered her home.

THE LAST YEARS IN RWANDA

Fossey returned to Karisoke in June of 1983. Her return was covered by reporters, photographers, and television filmmakers. The Rwandan government recognized her for her contributions to science and the local economy. When they all had left and Fossey had settled in, the camp director, Richard Barnes, began to realize that this was no brief visit. The camp's staff hoped that the trip to America and the respite in Maine had taken the bite from Fossey's fury toward the poachers, but it soon became obvious that the Gorilla Girl had not changed.

She immediately picked up just where she had left off, abusing and humiliating the native staff and hunting down poachers—interrogating, threatening, and even torturing them. The National Geographic Society, hearing of Fossey's behavior, discontinued her funding. But Fossey had been penniless before. She had never received any salary for her work, and operating funds had always been in short supply. Her

WHO KILLED DIAN FOSSEY?

The government charged one of Fossey's longtime trackers, Rwelakana, with her murder, some six months after the event. He was cleared, but only after he was found dead in his cell, apparently having hanged himself—though diplomats in Kigali suspected that he had actually died many weeks earlier, of beatings and torture by Rwandan officials. Wayne McGuire, one of two assistants in the camp that night, also was suspected, largely because he was the last to see Fossey alive. Warned by the U.S. Embassy of his impending arrest, McGuire left the country, claiming innocence, but he was tried and convicted anyway, *in absentia*.

Dr. Fossey's death remained a mystery until June of 2001, when the powerful politician Protais Zigiranyirazo—known in the region as "Mr. Z" or "Monsieur Zed"—was captured by Belgian police. The "death squads" that Zigiranyirazo had created after the death of his brother-in-law, former Rwandan president Juvenal Habyarimana, had killed about 500,000 people in ethnic massacres in 1994, and Zigiranyirazo was wanted internationally for war crimes.

Zigiranyirazo served as governor of Ruhengeri when Fossey was there. Many claim that Fossey intended to denounce his support of poaching and gold-smuggling operations in Rwanda, and that he masterminded the killing that silenced her. Zigiranyirazo's political connections may have shielded him for years, as his brother-in-law was president at the time of Fossey's death. But the protection seems to have ended when Mr. Zigiranyirazo was arrested in 2001.

favorite uncle, Bert, had bequeathed $50,000 to her, money she had spent to keep the camp running. Now, she used the royalties from *Gorillas in the Mist*, combined with contributions to the Digit Fund, to continue her patrols. She paid men to cut all snares and traps they found, and to bring all suspected poachers to her. She kept up the pace despite her dwindling energy. Her face was haggard and puffy, she had begun to cough up blood, and those who knew her believed she was dying. But her work continued.

Just before Christmas of 1985, Dr. Fossey hung her decorations as usual. Sometime during the night of December 26 she was murdered. Her body was placed in a sleeping bag and carried down the mountain, where it was preserved in ice at a local brewery until funeral arrangements could be made.

Although Fossey had left written instructions that she be buried in the small gorilla cemetery behind her cabin, her stepfather, Richard Price, initially opposed the idea; but officials at the U.S. Embassy finally persuaded him to respect Fossey's wishes. On the morning of December 31, 1985, Fossey's body was placed in a plain wooden coffin, and she made her last trip up Mount Visoke. Wayne McGuire asked some members of Karisoke's staff to dig Fossey's grave next to Digit's. Checking on their progress, he was horrified to find they had dug a very shallow grave in the dark, volcanic soil. He wanted the grave dug to a depth of six full feet. To trick them into continuing to dig, he told them that it was the American custom to dig until the minister arrived. They kept digging and finished just before the arrival of the funeral procession.

The procession included some of Fossey's friends and associates, including Amy Vedder, a primatologist who had come to Karisoke to study the gorillas in 1973; Joan Root; and Rosamond Carr. For the grief-stricken Carr, 75, the climb was arduous. Reverend Elton Wallace, a Seventh-Day Adventist minister, had been asked to lead the service. When the procession reached Karisoke, it was joined by the camp's workers.

"NYIRAMACHABELLI"

DIAN FOSSEY

1932 — 1985

NO ONE LOVED GORILLAS MORE

REST IN PEACE, DEAR FRIEND

ETERNALLY PROTECTED

IN THIS SACRED GROUND

FOR YOU ARE HOME

WHERE YOU BELONG

As her grave marker suggests, Fossey found a home among the gorillas of the Virungas and became the very center of life at Karisoke.

It was a beautiful morning, eight years to the day since Digit had been murdered. Now Fossey joined her friend in his resting place. The group of mourners stood beneath a clear sky as Rev. Wallace delivered the homily of scriptures. Rosamond

Carr wept as she stood among the silent mourners. When the minister finished the service, Carr laid an assortment of flowers from her plantation on her long-time friend's casket. Amy Vedder had gathered an assortment of the gorillas' favorite plants, including thistles and wild celery. She laid her bouquet next to Carr's.

Karisoke still exists, though it has been evacuated, destroyed, and rebuilt several times due to political turmoil. Tourists still come to see the mountain gorillas and visit Fossey's grave. Some of them enjoy the thrill of being touched by one of the descendants of Dian Fossey's family, for the gorillas remain as trusting of humans as she taught them to be. The Digit Fund and other organizations have raised enough money to pay for effective patrols to curb poaching.

Five years after Dian Fossey's death, the mountain gorilla population stopped declining and began to increase. And that may be her greatest legacy, for, as her tombstone reads, "no one loved gorillas more."

Chronology

1932   Dian Fossey is born on January 16 near San Francisco, the only child of George and Kitty Fossey.

1949   Graduates from high school. Studies business at Marin Junior College.

1950   Enters University of California at Davis as pre-veterinary major.

1954   Receives B.A. in Occupational Therapy from San Jose State College.

1956   Hired as Director of occupational therapy, Kosair Children's Hospital, Louisville, Kentucky.

1963   First visits Africa in September. Meets Louis Leakey; sees first gorillas; returns to Kosair Children's Hospital; meets Dr. Leakey again in Louisville; obtains grant to work in Africa.

1966   Returns to Africa. Begins field study at Kabara, in Congo (later Zaire, now the Democratic Republic of the Congo).

1967   Establishes Karisoke Research Center with one employee in Volcanoes National Park, Rwanda.

1968   First structure built at Karisoke.

1969   Nurses gorilla infants Coco and Pucker back to health at Karisoke.

1970   Peanuts touches Fossey's hand; *National Geographic* cover story; Fossey begins study at Cambridge University in Cambridge, England. "Making Friends with Mountain Gorillas" (article).

1971   "More Years with Mountain Gorillas" (article).

1974   Receives Ph.D. in zoology.

1978   Digit and Uncle Bert (gorilla) are killed; Digit Fund created.

1980   Resigns directorship of Karisoke; becomes visiting associate professor at Cornell University in Ithaca, New York.

1981   "The Imperiled Mountain Gorilla" (article).

1983   Returns to Karisoke as Director in June; *Gorillas in the Mist* published.

1985   Murdered at Karisoke, December 26.

1988   Motion picture *Gorillas in the Mist* is released, starring Sigourney Weaver as Dian Fossey.

1990s   Karisoke closed several times due to war; Fossey's cabin is burned.

1997   Karisoke Research Center fully operational.

Bibliography

Ake, Ann. *The Gorilla.* San Diego: Lucent, 1999.

Brower, Montgomery, and Maryanne Vollers. "The Strange Death of Dian Fossey." *People Weekly* (Feb. 17, 1986), 46.

Carr, Rosamond Halsey. *Land of a Thousand Hills: My Life in Rwanda.* New York: Penguin, 1999.

Croke, Vicki. "Man of the Wild." *Animals,* Winter 2002.

Dreifus, Claudia. "Jane of the Jungle." *Modern Maturity,* Dec/Nov 1999.

Fossey, Dian. *Gorillas in the Mist.* Boston: Houghton Mifflin, 1983.

———. "The Imperiled Mountain Gorilla." *National Geographic,* Apr. 1981.

———. "Making Friends with Mountain Gorillas." *National Geographic,* Jan. 1970.

———. "More Years with Mountain Gorillas." *National Geographic,* Oct. 1971.

Freedman, Suzanne. *Dian Fossey: Befriending the Gorillas.* Austin: Raintree/Steck Vaughan, 1997.

Goodall, Jane. *Beyond Innocence: An Autobiography in Letters: The Later Years.* Boston: Houghton Mifflin, 2001.

———. *Through a Window: My Thirty Years with the Chimpanzees of Gombe.* Boston: Houghton Mifflin, 1990.

Gordon, Nicholas. *Murders in the Mist: Who Killed Dian Fossey?* London: Hodder & Stoughton, 1993.

———. "Gorillas in the Lens." *Buzzworm,* Jan./Feb. 1993.

Hayes, Harold T.P. *The Dark Romance of Dian Fossey.* New York: Simon & Schuster, 1990.

Jerome, Leah. *Dian Fossey.* New York: Bantam, 1991.

Johanson, Donald C. "The Leakey Family." *Time* (Mar. 29, 1999).

McBee, Susanna. "Great Apes Get New Lease on Life." *U.S. News and World Report* (Jun. 9, 1986).

McGuire, Wayne. "I Didn't Kill Fossey. She Was My Friend." *Discover,* Feb. 1997.

Montgomery, Sy. *Walking with the Great Apes: Jane Goodall, Dian Fossey, Birute Galdikas.* Boston: Houghton Mifflin, 1991.

Morell, Virginia. "Dian Fossey: Field Science and Death in Africa." *Science,* Apr. 1986.

———, Patricia Kahn, Toomas Koppel, and Dennis Normile. "Called 'Trimates,' Three Bold Women Shaped Their Field." *Science* (Apr. 16, 1993), 420.

Mowat, Farley. *Woman in the Mists: The Story of Dian Fossey and the Mountain Gorillas of Africa.* New York: Warner Books, 1987.

Peterson, Dale. *The Deluge and the Dark: A Journey into Primate Worlds.* Boston: Houghton Mifflin, 1989.

Prince-Hughes, Dawn. *Gorillas Among Us: A Primate Ethnographer's Book of Days.* University of Arizona, 2001.

Roberts, Jack. *Dian Fossey.* San Diego: Lucent, 1995.

"Satellite to Spy on Gorillas." *Geographical,* Dec. 2002.

Schaller, George B. "Gentle Gorillas, Turbulent Times." *National Geographic* (Oct. 1995), 66.

———, and Tom Matthews. *Light Shining Through the Mist: A Photobiography of Dian Fossey.* Washington: National Geographic Society, 1998.

Schott, Jane A. *Dian Fossey and the Mountain Gorillas.* Minneapolis: Carolrhoda, 2000.

Sheppard, R.Z. "Gorillas in the Mist." *Time* (Aug. 15, 1983).

Smita, Paul. "Mates in Peril." *Animals,* Winter 2001.

"Unnatural Death." *Time* (Jan. 13, 1986).

Weaver, Sigourney. "Queen Kong." *Life,* Oct. 1988.

Weber, Bill, and Amy Vedder. *In the Kingdom of Gorillas: Fragile Species in a Dangerous Land.* New York: Simon & Schuster, 2001.

"Zoologist Is Slain in Central Africa." *The New York Times* (Dec. 29, 1985), 6.

Works by Dian Fossey

"Making Friends with Mountain Gorillas." *National Geographic,* January 1970.

"More Years with Mountain Gorillas." *National Geographic,* October 1971.

"The Imperiled Mountain Gorilla." *National Geographic,* April 1981.

Gorillas in the Mist. Boston: Houghton Mifflin, 1983.

Further Reading

Ake, Ann. *The Gorilla*. San Diego: Lucent, 1999.

Fossey, Dian. *Gorillas in the Mist*. Boston: Houghton Mifflin, 1983.

———. "The Imperiled Mountain Gorilla." *National Geographic*, Apr. 1981.

———. "Making Friends with Mountain Gorillas." *National Geographic*, Jan. 1970.

———. "More Years with Mountain Gorillas." *National Geographic*, Oct. 1971.

Freedman, Suzanne. *Dian Fossey: Befriending the Gorillas*. Austin, Texas: Raintree/Steck Vaughan, 1997.

Jerome, Leah. *Dian Fossey*. New York: Bantam, 1991.

Matthews, Tom. *Light Shining Through the Mist: A Photobiography of Dian Fossey*. Washington, DC: National Geographic Society. 1998.

Mowat, Farley. *Virunga: Passion Dian Fossey*. Toronto: McClelland & Stewart, 1987.

Roberts, Jack. *Dian Fossey*. San Diego: Lucent Books, 1995.

Rowe, Noel. *The Pictorial Guide to Living Primates*. East Hampton, New York: Pogonias Press, 1996.

Sapolsky, Robert M. *A Primate's Memoir*. Touchstone Books, 2002.

Schaller, George B., and Michael Nichols (photographer). *Gorilla: Struggle for Survival in the Wilderness*. Aperture: 1989. Paperback edition 1992.

———. *The Mountain Gorilla: Ecology and Behavior*. University of Chicago Press, 1963. Paperback edition 1989.

———. *The Year of the Gorilla*. (Reissued.) University of Chicago Press, 1997.

Films

Gorilla, by National Geographic, 1976, 1981.

Gorillas in the Mist, Universal Studios, 1988.

Websites

The Dian Fossey Gorilla Fund International
www.gorillafund.org

The International Primate Protection League
www.ippl.org

The Gorilla Foundation
www.koko.org

The Ape Alliance
www.4apcs.com

The World Wide Gorilla Fund for Nature: "Apes"
www.panda.org/species/gorilla_east/

The Born Free Foundation's Primate Project
www.bornfree.org.uk/primate/index.html

The Louis S.B. Leakey Foundation
www.leakeyfoundation.org

The American Anthropological Association
www.aaanet.org

The Association for Women in Science
1200 New York Ave., Suite 650 NW
Washington, DC USA 20005
202.326.8940
www.awis.org

Index

Index

Picture Credits

page:

13: © Dian Fossey Gorilla Foundation International (DFGFI)
16: © Yann Arthus-Bertrand/CORBIS
19: © Yann Arthus-Bertrand/CORBIS
21: Associated Press, AP
33: Courtesy CIA
40: Associated Press, AP
47: © DFGFI

49: © Robert Maass/CORBIS
56: © Yann Arthus-Bertrand/CORBIS
61: © DFGFI
63: © Hulton-Archive/Getty Images, Inc.
69: Associated Press, AP
72: © DFGFI
75: © DFGFI
78: © Joe McDonald/CORBIS

83: © DFGFI
84: Associated Press, AP
87: © DFGFI
94: © Yann Arthus-Bertrand/CORBIS
97: © Yann Arthus-Bertrand/CORBIS
99: © DFGFI
103: Associated Press, AP
108: © DFGFI

Contributors

LOIS P. NICHOLSON is a school library media specialist at Stevensville Middle School in Stevensville, Maryland. She holds a bachelor's degree in elementary education and a master's degree in education, both from Salisbury State University. As a school librarian and as an author, she emphasizes the importance of students reading a variety of literature, including nonfiction titles that correspond to their reading interests. She is the author of 15 books for young adults, including 11 titles for Chelsea House. Lois is the mother of two grown children and lives with her husband, Norman L. Macht—also an author for Chelsea House—in Easton, Maryland.

JILL SIDEMAN, PH.D. serves as vice president of CH2M HILL, an international environmental-consulting firm based in San Francisco. She was among the few women to study physical chemistry and quantum mechanics in the late 1960s and conducted over seven years of post-doctoral research in high-energy physics and molecular biology. In 1974, she co-founded a woman-owned environmental-consulting firm that became a major force in environmental-impact analysis, wetlands and coastal zone management, and energy conservation. She went on to become Director of Environmental Planning and Senior Client Service Manager at CH2M HILL. An active advocate of women in the sciences, she was elected in 2001 as president of the Association for Women in Science, a national organization "dedicated to achieving equity and full participation for women in science, mathematics, engineering and technology.".